EYEWITNESS
ISLAM

A poetry reading

7th-century coin, minted when the Umayyad dynasty ruled from Damascus, Syria

Water jug presented to Charlemagne by 8th-century caliph, Harun al-Rashid

Mosque finial of Selimiye Mosque, Turkey

Arabic quadrant, for measuring the height of stars, with instructions

Lute decorated with traditional Islamic patterns

Star lantern

Map of the world by Moroccan-born writer and geographer, al-Idrisi (1099–1180)

Guidebook to the hajj (the pilgrimage)

EYEWITNESS
ISLAM

Written by
Philip Wilkinson

Editorial Consultant
Batul Salazar

The Qutb Minar, Delhi, India

Bedouin wearing
traditional costume

Prayer beads

Ubudiah Mosque, Malaysia

Gold bracelet

13th-century book illustration of
Ramadan procession

DK

Islamic star-shaped
decorative tile

A book rest
supporting a copy
of the Quran

THIRD EDITION
DK DELHI
Project editor Janashree Singha
Art editor Revati Anand
Senior DTP designer Harish Aggarwal
DTP designers Pawan Kumar, Rakesh Kumar
Jacket designer Tanya Mehrotra
Jackets editorial coordinator Priyanka Sharma
Managing jackets editor Saloni Singh
Pre-production manager Balwant Singh
Production manager Pankaj Sharma
Managing editor Kingshuk Ghoshal
Managing art editor Govind Mittal

DK LONDON
Senior editors Ann Baggaley, Camilla Hallinan
US editor Megan Douglass **US executive editor** Lori Cates Hand
Senior art editor Spencer Holbrook
Jacket designer Surabhi Wadhwa-Gandhi **Jacket editor** Claire Gell
Jacket design development manager Sophia MTT
Producer, pre-production Jennifer Murray
Senior producer Angela Graef
Managing editor Francesca Baines
Managing art editor Philip Letsu
Publisher Andrew Macintyre
Associate publishing director Liz Wheeler
Art director Karen Self **Design director** Phil Ormerod
Publishing director Jonathan Metcalf
Consultant Andrew Humphreys

FIRST EDITION
Project editor Kitty Blount **Art editor** Clair Watson
Editor Francesca Baines **Production** Kate Oliver
Special photography Steve Teague
Picture research Angela Anderson, Alex Pepper,
Deborah Pownall, and Sarah Pownall
DTP designer Siu Yin Ho **Jacket designer** Dean Price

Two of the Rightly Guided Caliphs,
Companions of the Prophet

10th-century Arabic copy of
an herbal encyclopedia by the
Greek surgeon Dioscorides

Bronze bird from Persia

Saudi Arabian
woman wearing
a face veil

Coffee pot

A WORLD OF IDEAS:
SEE ALL THERE IS TO KNOW

www.dk.com

A caravan of pilgrims, including a camel
carrying a pavilion called a *mahmal*

16th-century painting of
Muslim astronomers

Contents

Mamluk mosque lamp

Early Arabia   6

The Prophet Muhammad   8

The Quran   10

The Five Pillars of Islam   12

The mosque   18

The caliphate   20

First conquests   22

Scholars and teachers   24

Spreading ideas   28

On the move   32

Islamic culture   34

The Islamic city   36

Trade and travel   38

The Crusades   42

Arms and armor   44

Spain   46

Africa   48

Mongols and Turks   50

Central Asia, Iran,
    and India   52

The Far East   54

Costume and jewelry   56

Islamic society   58

Festivals   60

Did you know?   64

Find out more   66

Glossary   68

The Alhambra Palace   70

Index and
    acknowledgments   72

Early Arabia

The Arabian Peninsula was home to advanced cultures long before the birth of Muhammad, the Prophet of Islam, in the 6th century. Arabia's position at a crossroads between Asia, Africa, and Europe enriched her traders. Most Arab tribes worshipped their own idols, while Christians and Jews worshipped one God. The Prophet offered the word of the One God in the Quran, in their own language, and a new religion called Islam.

South Arabic inscription
The kings of Saba (biblical Sheba) ruled southern Arabia between the 8th and 2nd centuries BCE. Archaeologists have found many inscriptions in the Sabaeans' angular script, which passed out of use after they lost power.

Date harvest
Settlements grew up at small oases across the Arabian Peninsula. Here there was a reliable water supply and date palms grew, providing a succulent harvest for the local people.

Desert dunes
Much of Arabia is harsh desert, vast expanses of either sand or rock. The name Arab means "desert nomad"—many Arabs adopted a nomadic way of life, roaming with their flocks in order to find water and survive.

Dramatic rocks
This startling rock formation rises from the stony desert of Jiddat al-Harasis, in Oman. The most fertile part of Arabia is Yemen, which gets monsoon rains from the Indian Ocean.

Palmyra
The city of Palmyra in the Syrian desert was an oasis where key trade routes met. Its art and architecture combined both Greek and Roman styles, as seen in this figure of a woman, and local traditions.

The Arab world

The Arabian Peninsula lies between the Red Sea and the Persian Gulf. Arab peoples built towns in the fertile area of Yemen, at oases, and on the coasts. To the northeast, the Sasanid Empire of the Persians occupied Iran. To the northwest lay the Christian Byzantine Empire.

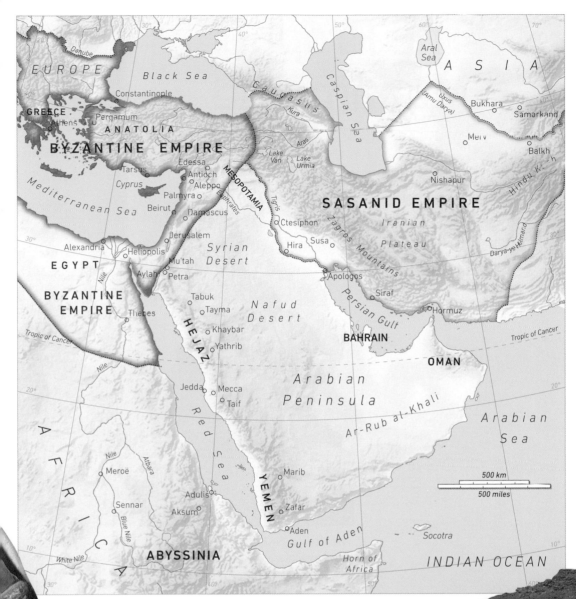

The Arab world at the time of the birth of the Prophet Muhammad in 570

Altar for burning frankincense

Precious perfume

Frankincense was one of Arabia's most prized and widely traded products. Trade routes crisscrossed the peninsula and many of its early cities, such as the Nabatean town of Petra (in modern Jordan), grew up along the roads.

Walls at Marib

Marib, in Yemen, was the capital city of the Sabaeans, and some of its ancient walls survive. Marib was built on a trade route and grew into a large, thriving city, with a palace (home of the Queen of Sheba) and many houses. There was also a famous dam, an amazing feat of engineering for the 7th century BCE.

The Prophet Muhammad

Muhammad was born in 570 in the city of Mecca (in what is now Saudi Arabia). His mission as Prophet of Islam began in 610, when the Quran was first revealed to him. His teachings about the one God upset people in Mecca who worshipped many idols, so he eventually moved to the city of Medina, which became the center of a great Islamic civilization.

Archangel Gabriel

The Quran was revealed to Muhammad by the Archangel Gabriel, the angel of revelation. On an occasion known as the Night of Destiny, the revelation began. Then the Quran was communicated in small parts over a number of years.

Many names

Tradition gives the Prophet 200 names, including Habib Allah (Beloved of God) and Miftah al-Jannah (Key of Paradise). Usually when Muslims refer to Muhammad, they add the phrase *alayhi as-salam* (peace be upon him).

The word "Muhammad" written in calligraphy

The life of a trader

As a young man, Muhammad became a merchant and worked for a wealthy widow called Khadija. He traveled with camel caravans along the trading routes that crisscrossed Arabia and linked the peninsula with the Mediterranean and the Indian Ocean. Khadija was impressed with Muhammad, and, although she was considerably older than him, the two married.

Jabal al-Nur

Every year, during the month of Ramadan, Muhammad retired to Jabal al-Nur (the Mountain of Light) a few miles from Mecca to pray, fast, and give to the poor. It was here that the Prophet received the first revelation of the Quran.

The name "Muhammad" in stylized form

The Prophet

The Prophet of Islam, Muhammad is seen by Muslims as the last of a series of prophets, including Abraham, Moses, and Jesus, all of whom were mortal.

Mountain retreat

At the top of Jabal al-Nur, Muhammad stayed in a cave called Hira. The cave was quite small, but it faced toward Mecca and had enough space for Muhammad to pray. One of his daughters brought him food so that he could stay in the cave for the whole month of Ramadan.

Star pattern based on "Allah" in Arabic script

Allah

Allah is the name of the one God in whom Muslims believe and upon whom all life and existence depends. He is unique and infinitely greater than any thing He has created. The Quran says that He is "unbegotten"—having no origin and no end, He is and always will be.

The Prophet's Mosque in Medina

Medina

Muhammad was persecuted in his native Mecca, but in 622, people from the city of Yathrib, later called Medina, to the north of Mecca invited him to go and live there. The Prophet and his followers' migration, known as the Hijrah, marks the start of the Islamic era. Eventually he defeated the pagans in Mecca and cleared the idols from the Kaba, so Islam could flourish there, too.

Muhammad's face is veiled because Islam does not allow him to be depicted.

The Archangel Gabriel

The Night Journey

One night, the Archangel Gabriel woke Muhammad and led him to a steed called Buraq. It carried the Prophet overnight from Mecca to Jerusalem, where he ascended to heaven.

Buraq is always depicted with a human face.

Muhammad's tomb

The Prophet died in the lap of his favorite wife, Aisha, in her apartment near the mosque at Medina. His tomb was built where he died. Later, his close Companions Abu Bakr and Umar, the first two caliphs, were buried on either side.

Pattern based on names of the Companions

Companions

The Prophet's Companions were his closest followers. They memorized and passed the Quran on to others before it was written down.

The Quran

Starting in 610, the Archangel Gabriel revealed the Quran, the holy book of Islam, to the Prophet Muhammad over 22 years. Muslims believe that the Quran is Allah's final revelation to humanity and completes the sacred writings of the Jews and Christians but with Allah's actual words. Muslims first learned the words by heart, and later also wrote them down, and they aim to live by the Quran.

Quran container
This beautiful inlaid box is designed to hold a copy of the Quran divided into 30 sections. One section is read on each night of Ramadan, the month of fasting.

Bold Kufic script

Kufic script
Arabic has several types of script—the earliest is Kufic, from the town of Kufah (in modern Iraq). This example of eastern Kufic is from a copy of the Quran written out before the year 1000. The angular but elegant script has long upright and horizontal strokes.

Eastern Kufic script

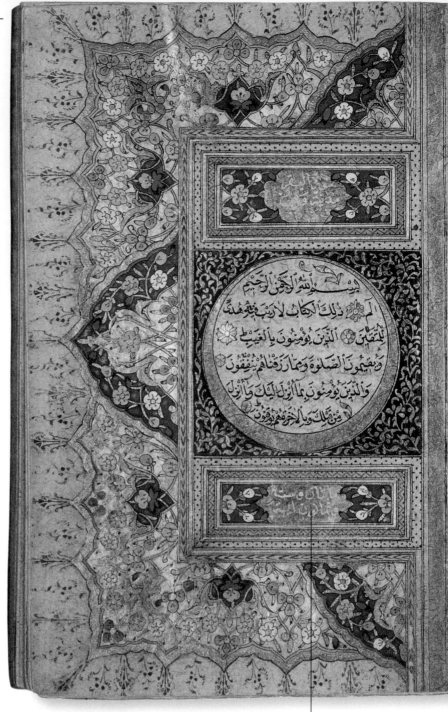

Decorated Quran
This copy of the Quran is open at the beginning of one of its 114 chapters, or *suras*. Each *sura* has a name that comes from a notable word that occurs in its text.

This box gives the number of verses in the sura. *The box at the top gives the name of the* sura.

"Praise belongs to Allah, the Lord of the worlds, the Merciful, the Compassionate, the Master of the Day of Judgement. Thee only do we serve; to Thee alone we pray for help. Guide us on the straight path, the path of those whom Thou hast blessed, not of those against whom Thou are wrathful, nor of those who are astray."

SURA AL-FATIHA, OPENING CHAPTER, THE QURAN

The text on this page is the opening chapter, Sura al-Fatiha, which is translated below to the left.

On a gemstone

In the eyes of a Muslim, this gemstone has been made far more valuable as it has a Quranic inscription on it, which is translated below.

"Allah—there is no god but He, the Living, the Everlasting. Slumber seizes Him not, neither sleep; to Him belongs all that is in the heavens and the earth ..."

AYAT AL-KURSI, THRONE VERSE, THE QURAN

On a tile

Muslims everywhere learn Arabic, the language of the Quran, and all over the Muslim world beautifully written quotations from the Quran are used for artistic decoration.

In a mushaf

When people refer to "the Quran," they usually mean a book that has the Quran written in it. Originally, the Quran was only recited and Muslims learned it by heart. The later, written version was called a *mushaf*, or a collection of pages. A *mushaf* will usually indicate whether each *sura* was revealed at Mecca or Medina.

Writing it down

Copying the text of the Quran is something that must be done with care and reverence—none of Allah's words must be altered. To make a hand-written copy of the Quran like this is an activity of great religious devotion.

The Five Pillars of Islam

There are five fundamental requirements of Islam, called the Five Pillars of Islam. First and foremost is the Shahada—the profession of faith. Islam, which means "submission" and comes from the word "peace," is considered by Muslims to restate the same truth—belief in the one God—that was revealed to Christians and Jews. The remaining four Pillars of Islam require all Muslims to pray, give alms, fast, and make the pilgrimage to Mecca.

Crescent moon and star

A crescent moon with a star was used as a symbol by the Turks in the 15th century and has since become the symbol of Islam. The words of the Shahada in Arabic calligraphy have been used here to form the shape of the moon, while Allah's title forms the star.

"In the name of Allah, the Merciful, the Compassionate."

Shahada

The Muslim profession of faith is called the Shahada. The English translation of the Shahada is: "There is no god but God; Muhammad is the messenger of God." Muslims use the Arabic word for God, which is "Allah," but they are referring to the same God that is worshipped by Christians and Jews. The words of the Shahada are heard often in the Muslim world—repeated during the daily calls to prayer, they are also whispered in a baby's ear at birth, and again at the time of a person's death.

Prayer

Muslims must pray at five set times during the day. These prayers, known as *salat*, make up the second Pillar of Islam. Muslims may pray on their own or in a group, but every Friday at midday, Muslim men must gather together for *salat al-jumaa*, or Friday prayers, led by an imam ("one who stands in front"), who will also give a sermon, or *khutba*.

Considered equal in the eyes of Allah, all members of the community perform the same rituals of ablution and prayer.

Rise up for prayer

Five times each day, the *adhan*, or call to prayer, is heard in Muslim communities. The times for prayer are between first light and sunrise (*fajr*), just after noon (*zuhr*), in late afternoon (*asr*), after sunset (*maghrib*), and evening (*isha*). The traditional practice is for an official called a *muezzin* to make the call from a minaret.

Preparing for prayer

Before prayer, a Muslim must rid the mind of distracting thoughts and cleanse the body. Ritual washing, or ablution, is done with running water at a fountain at the mosque or a tap and basin in the home—or with sand or a stone if in the desert.

In the direction of Mecca
To face the Kaba in Mecca during prayers, Muslims need to know the direction, *qibla*, of the city. In the Middle Ages, people made compasses that pointed to Mecca. In mosques, a niche, *mihrab*, in the wall shows which direction to face.

Qibla indicator

Prayer beads
Allah is referred to in many different ways, known as *al-asma al-husna*, the 99 beautiful names. The string of 99 beads that a Muslim uses in private prayer is a reminder of the 99 Divine names.

Prayer mat
The majority of Muslims pray on a mat, and some people take this with them wherever they go, so that they are always able to use It. Prayer rugs are often beautifully made, but any mat, from a silk rug to a piece of reed matting, may be used. It is also quite permissible to pray on the uncovered ground, provided that it is clean.

Prayer beads may be used to repeat the 99 beautiful names, or to repeat other phrases used in prayer.

Iranian prayer mat

1 The raka begins
The words Allahu Akbar—Allah is greater (than all else)—open the *raka*. Then Allah is praised, and the first *sura*, or chapter, of the Quran, called *al-Fatiha*—the Opening—is spoken, together with a second *sura*.

5 Peace
In the final *salam*, or peace, the person looks left and right, and then says, "Peace be with you and the mercy of Allah," addressing all present, seen and unseen.

4 Sitting
This position, *julus*, is for a short silent prayer. Then the prostration is repeated, ending with a prayer for the community and for the worshipper's sins to be forgiven.

3 Prostration
This position, *sujud*, shows humility, while saying silently, "Glory to my Lord the Most High. Allah is greater."

2 Bowing down
After another passage from the Quran is recited, bowing, *ruku*, shows respect for Allah and is followed by *qiyam*, standing and praising Allah.

Stages of prayer
Prayer follows a precise order of words and motions. Each unit, or *raka*, consists of several stages. During prayers, the *raka* is repeated two, three, or four times, depending on which of the five daily prayers is being performed.

Continued from previous page

Almsgiving

The giving of alms (gifts) to the poor and needy is very important in Islam. Of all the ways in which one can give to the poor, the most formal is by paying a tax called *zakat*, which is one of the Five Pillars of Islam. The amount of *zakat* that a person has to pay is worked out as a percentage of their wealth. The tax is distributed among the poor and may also be used to help other needy members of society.

Water supply

In addition to paying *zakat*, a person may make other personal donations to help the community. These can provide useful facilities such as this public drinking fountain in Istanbul, Turkey. Many Muslim countries are in dry areas in which water can be hard to come by, so giving money for a fountain is especially useful.

Public baths

Hygiene is very important in Islam. Bath houses are a common sight in towns, and are often paid for by donations. A typical public bath has a changing room, often roofed with a shallow dome, and a series of rooms at different temperatures. The hottest is the steam room, for working up a sweat before being cleaned and massaged.

Hospitals

The places where the sick are treated are another group of facilities paid for by almsgiving. This beautiful latticed window is part of a hospital originally financed with almsgiving. Medicine was one area in which the Muslim world made many advances before the West.

Money or goods

Zakat is commonly paid in money but may also be given in the form of goods. In both cases, rates of payment are laid down, starting at 2.5 percent of a person's wealth, excluding their home and other essential items. The word *zakat* means "purification," because it is believed that giving up part of your wealth purifies what remains. In some countries, people give *zakat* voluntarily, while in others, it is compulsory, and collected by the government.

Food for the poor

In some parts of Muslim India, large cooking pots, or *deghs*, are used to prepare food outdoors. At the shrine of Ajmer, two *deghs* are used to make food for the needy, and people visiting the shrine make charitable gifts of food for the pots.

For lasting good

This document details a gift made to the state for good works. This type of gift is known as a *waqf* and is put toward the upkeep of mosques and other public buildings such as hospitals.

A proper meal

During Ramadan, Muslims break their fast after sunset with a light snack, which may consist simply of a few dates with water. Sunset prayers are followed by a much bigger meal.

Joyful procession

When the great solemnity of the month of Ramadan comes to an end, there may be a procession. This illustration, from a 13th-century book from Baghdad, Iraq, shows a procession accompanied with trumpets and banners.

Fasting

Muhammad received the first revelation of the Quran during the month of Ramadan, and this month has a special significance in Islam. Every day during Ramadan, Muslims fast from dawn to sunset, avoiding food, drink, and sexual relations. Although this fast, or *sawm*, is one of the Pillars of Islam, not everyone has to go without food. For example, those who are too sick to fast, women who are pregnant, and very young children may be excused.

Signaling Ramadan

In many Muslim countries, cannons are fired before the first day of Ramadan, to signal the beginning of the month. They are also fired to signal the beginning and end of each day of Ramadan.

Ending Ramadan

The end of Ramadan is marked by the festival of Eid al-Fitr—the feast of the breaking of the fast. At the beginning of this festival, the whole community gathers at an outdoor prayer area (or at a mosque) to perform the Eid prayer. Celebrations last for three days, during which time alms are given to the poor, and friends may exchange gifts.

Continued on next page

Pilgrimage

The final Pillar of Islam is hajj, or pilgrimage. All Muslims aim to perform this "greater pilgrimage" once in their lives. It involves a series of rites that take place annually over several days at the Sacred Mosque at Mecca and the nearby areas of Mina, Muzdalifa, and Arafat. A shorter pilgrimage to Mecca, known as *umrah*, forms part of the hajj, but may be performed by itself at any time of the year.

At the Kaba

Upon arrival in Mecca, pilgrims perform *umrah*, circling the Kaba seven times and praying near the Station of Abraham. In memory of Hagar, mother of Abraham's eldest son, Ishmael, they then run between two small hills, Safa and Marwa, after drinking water from the well of Zamzam.

Hajj

After performing *umrah*, the pilgrims travel to the valley of Mina. On the second day, they go to Arafat and pray for forgiveness as a foretaste of the Day of Judgment, when they will rise from the dead, be judged by Allah, and enter paradise if worthy. On their way back, they stop at Muzdalifa and spend part of the night resting, praying, and gathering small pebbles before returning to Mina. On the third day, they throw seven of the pebbles at the largest of three stone pillars that represent the temptations of Satan. For the next two days, they throw more pebbles at the pillars. They also make an animal sacrifice, and then wash and clip or shave their hair to symbolize a new beginning, before returning to Mecca to make seven final circuits around the Kaba.

Piece of cloth from the Kaba

Cloths of the Kaba

The Kaba (below) is a stone building, about 43 ft (13 m) across, at the center of the Sacred Mosque at Mecca. It is an ancient sanctuary dedicated to God and is covered with a black cloth embroidered with verses from the Quran. Every year, the cloth is renewed and precious pieces of the old cloth (left) are given away.

Guidebook

An ancient guidebook to Mecca illustrates features of the Sacred Mosque. It shows the stepped *minbar*—the pulpit from which the sermon is preached—together with a hanging lamp made of precious metal.

Quotation from the Quran saying that the pilgrimage to Mecca is a duty for all who can make their way there

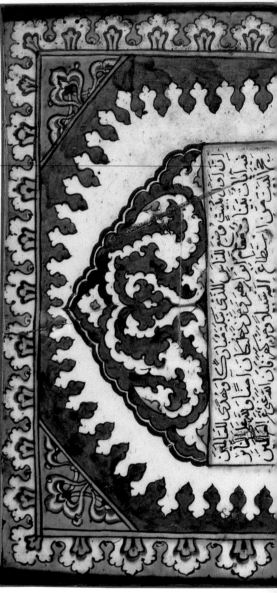

Tile with the Plan of the Sacred Mosque at Mecca, known in Arabic as the Masjid al-Haram

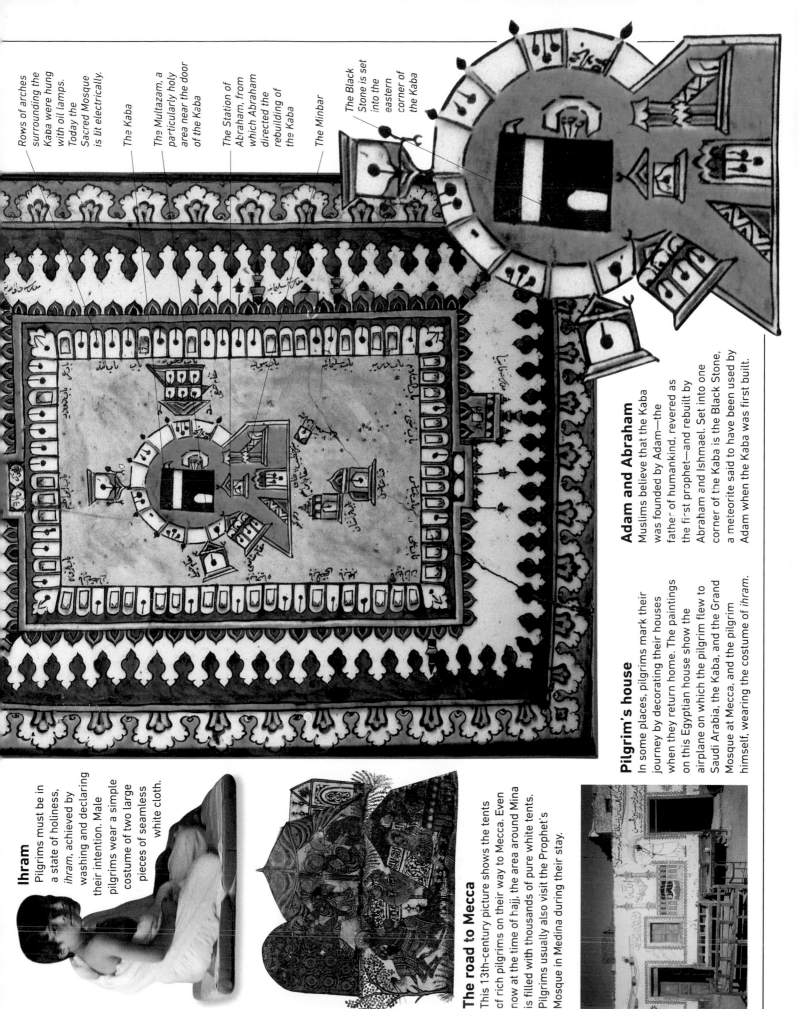

Rows of arches surrounding the Kaba were hung with oil lamps. Today the Sacred Mosque is lit electrically.

The Kaba

The Multazam, a particularly holy area near the door of the Kaba

The Station of Abraham, from which Abraham directed the rebuilding of the Kaba

The Minbar

The Black Stone is set into the eastern corner of the Kaba

Adam and Abraham

Muslims believe that the Kaba was founded by Adam—the father of humankind, revered as the first prophet—and rebuilt by Abraham and Ishmael. Set into one corner of the Kaba is the Black Stone, a meteorite said to have been used by Adam when the Kaba was first built.

Pilgrim's house

In some places, pilgrims mark their journey by decorating their houses when they return home. The paintings on this Egyptian house show the airplane on which the pilgrim flew to Saudi Arabia, the Kaba, and the Grand Mosque at Mecca, and the pilgrim himself, wearing the costume of *ihram*.

Ihram

Pilgrims must be in a state of holiness, *ihram*, achieved by washing and declaring their intention. Male pilgrims wear a simple costume of two large pieces of seamless white cloth.

The road to Mecca

This 13th-century picture shows the tents of rich pilgrims on their way to Mecca. Even now at the time of hajj, the area around Mina is filled with thousands of pure white tents. Pilgrims usually also visit the Prophet's Mosque in Medina during their stay.

The mosque

While every town has one main mosque, at which people gather for Friday prayers, mosques are open all through the week. Specifically used for prayer, they also provide places at which religious discussions can take place, and where education and charitable work can be organized. Most mosques serve their local area and form the spiritual center of the local community. Although they may be funded by wealthy donors, they are built and run by local people.

Centers of learning
Many big mosques have libraries that contain books on religious subjects, including Islamic law. In addition, mosques often have schools where children learn to memorize and recite the Quran.

Inside a mosque
Mosques vary enormously in design, from simple, plain rooms to vast ornate buildings—there is no one standard design. All that is really needed is a space in which the community can pray and some way of indicating the direction of Mecca. But there are standards of behavior and dress that must be observed inside every mosque. People take off their shoes and cover their heads before going in, and often an area of the mosque is reserved for women.

The courtyard is a place to meditate or read.

Entrance to mosque

A fountain or area for washing is found inside.

Prayer hall

Model of a mosque

Mosque dome

The mihrab is a niche indicating the direction of Mecca.

Prayer hall floor is covered with carpets.

Crescent finial

The call to prayer is given from the minaret.

British mosque
Mosques are often built in the local style of architecture, like this example in a British city.

Styles of minaret
The *muezzin* traditionally gives the call to prayer from the minaret, the highest point of a mosque. Minarets have been built in many styles and can be richly decorated or plain; square, many-sided, or round; slender or stocky.

Minaret of Samarra Great Mosque, Iraq

Minaret of Salihiye Mosque, Syria

Minaret of Tekkiye Mosque, Syria

Minbar
At Friday prayers the congregation listens to the *khutba*, a sermon given by the imam from a raised pulpit called the *minbar*. Some *minbars*, which can be beautifully adorned with inlay and carving, have survived from 1,000 years ago.

Oil lamp
Traditionally mosques were lit by oil lamps. These large, hanging lamps could be brightly decorated—like this example of bronze covered with gold and silver—to reflect the light and shine more brightly. People giving alms often donated money to pay for oil for the lamps.

15th-century mosque lamp

Mosque finial of Selimiye Mosque in Turkey

Elaborate tile decoration

The Blue Mosque in Istanbul
In 1453, the Ottomans took over Constantinople (modern Istanbul). The city's Christian churches were lavishly decorated and roofed with domes. Ottoman architects built their mosques in a similar style.

Sydney mosque
The first Muslims to reach Australia were Afghan and Punjabi camel drivers, arriving between 1867 and 1918 to provide rural transport.

African mosque
This 16th-century African mosque has a very simple design. The style of the building, however, is not significant in a mosque. Its function as a meeting place to pray is the most important thing.

Mosque decoration
As Muslims prospered, they could adorn their mosques with sumptuous decoration, like these tiles on a minaret in Turkey. Carpets for the prayer hall were another favorite gift.

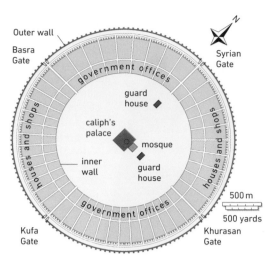

Outer wall
Basra Gate
Syrian Gate
N
government offices
guard house
caliph's palace
mosque
inner wall
guard house
houses and shops
houses and shops
government offices
500 m
500 yards
Kufa Gate
Khurasan Gate

The caliphate

When the Prophet Muhammad died in 632, leading Muslims gathered to elect Abu Bakr as *khalifa* (caliph), which means "successor" or "viceroy." Others, however, favored the Prophet's cousin Ali, who had married his daughter Fatima, and they became known as Shia Muslims, or "supporters" of Ali. In 656, Ali became caliph, but Muslims were still divided: Sunni supported the system of an elected caliphate, while Shia believed the caliphs should be descended from Ali and Fatima.

The round city of Baghdad

The first Caliphate dynasty was the Rashidun, in 632–661. The Umayyad dynasty of 661–750 ruled from Damascus, Syria. They were replaced by the Abbasid caliphs who ruled for more than 500 years from their capital in Baghdad, Iraq. Founded in 762, the city was laid out as a circle, its gates aligned with the compass points, like a map of the Universe.

The role of the caliph

The caliph was expected to rule the Muslim world in accordance with Islamic principles. He also gave authority to local Muslim leaders, such as the powerful Mamluk sultanate that ruled in Egypt until the 16th century. This is a Mamluk mosque lamp, decorated with script from the *Sura al-Nur* of the Quran.

"Allah is the Light of the heavens and the Earth; the likeness of His Light is as a niche wherein is a lamp."

SURA AL-NUR, LIGHT CHAPTER, THE QURAN

The first caliphs

Abu Bakr, Umar, Uthman, and Ali were the first four caliphs and are greatly revered. As close Companions of the Prophet, they followed his example and are known as the Rightly Guided Caliphs.

Zulfiqar, the twin-bladed sword of Ali

Early caliph

Representation of living creatures is discouraged in Islam—only Allah has the divine right of creation—but this early portrait of a caliph is in a style imitated from pre-Islamic Persian coins.

Caliph's gift
The powerful 8th-century caliph Harun al-Rashid exchanged gifts with the Frankish emperor Charlemagne in western Europe, sending him this jeweled jug and an elephant.

Calligraphy reads, "Allah, Muhammad, Fatima, and Ali, Hasan, and Husayn"

Repeating calligraphic inscription

Tiraz
The Shia Fatimid caliphs of Cairo gave courtiers, ambassadors, and foreign rulers robes or lengths of cloth—*tiraz*—woven with calligraphy. Inscribed with the caliphs' names, Islamic prayers, or poems, they were highly prized.

Shia battle standard
In 680 at Kerbala, the army of the Umayyad caliph killed Husayn, son of Ali and Fatima, whose Shia forces carried the battle standard above. The events at Kerbala divided Shia and Sunni Muslims still more deeply. Today, around one tenth of all Muslims are Shia.

Protection for pilgrims
The caliph had to protect the holy cities of Mecca and Medina and the pilgrims traveling there, often with camels laden with gifts.

Inscription proclaiming the unity of Allah

Umayyad coin
This coin was minted by an Umayyad caliph in Damascus, Syria. After defeat by the Abbasids, an Umayyad offshoot ruled Muslim lands in the West from Spain.

Atatürk
The last caliphs were the Ottoman rulers of Turkey. In 1923, Turkey's first president, Kemal Atatürk, came to power. He decided to modernize his country and abolished the caliphate in 1924.

First conquests

The first three caliphs rapidly expanded their territory, creating an empire that eventually stretched from the Arabian Peninsula to Spain. Islam was spread by military conquest, but also by peaceful alliances with local rulers. Non-Muslims in these areas—Jews, Christians, and others—paid a tax and became known as *dhimmis* (the protected).

Expanding empire

By the end of the third caliphate in 656, the empire included Arabia, Palestine, Syria, Egypt, Libya, Iraq, large parts of Persia (Iran), and Sind (Pakistan). The Umayyad dynasty (661–750) expanded into the rest of North Africa and Spain and pushed eastward.

Crown and cross

This crown was made for a 7th-century Visigoth king in Spain, just before the Muslim invasion.

Rock of Gibraltar

Muslim forces landed in Spain in 711, arriving first on the Rock of Gibraltar under their commander, a Berber former slave, Tariq, from whom Gibraltar takes its name (Jebel Tariq). By 715, they had taken over most of Spain, settling mainly in the south, and soon their armies were entering France.

Map of Jerusalem

This mosaic map shows Jerusalem in the 6th century. The Muslims conquered the city in 638, during the reign of caliph Umar. For many centuries, Islamic rulers governed Jerusalem in a way that was tolerant of the Jews and Christians who lived there and who regarded it as a holy place.

Great Mosque

Under the Umayyad dynasty, the city of Damascus in Syria became the capital of the Islamic empire. The Umayyads built the Great Mosque in the early 8th century.

Mosque decoration

Mosques were built all around the empire, and many were lavishly decorated. This arch, above a doorway at the Great Mosque in Damascus, shows how Muslim stone masons used different marbles, together with inlays and mosaics made of other brightly colored stones.

22

Ruins of Carthage

The North African city of Carthage, originally home of the Phoenicians, was ruled by the Romans and later the Christian Byzantine Empire. In 697–698, Carthage fell to Muslim armies. The native Berber population soon accepted Islam and joined the westward drive of the Muslim forces.

Roman triumphal arch, Carthage

Charles Martel, King of the Franks

In the 8th century, much of western Europe was ruled by a Germanic people called the Franks under their king, Charles Martel. In 1732, he defeated the Muslim army at Tours, France, which marked the north-western limit of the Muslim empire, and soon drove the Muslims out of southern France.

Out in force

This image from an early manuscript shows Muslim soldiers gathering near their tents. Soldiers like these, efficient and well disciplined, were greatly feared in western Europe and advanced as far as France.

Almohad battle standard

In 1212, there was a battle at Navas de Tolosa, Spain, between a Christian army and the Almohads, the local Muslim dynasty. The Almohads, who marched behind this standard, were defeated, and Muslim power in Spain was weakened.

23

Scholars and teachers

Learning has always played a huge part in the Islamic world. Children learned to memorize and recite the text of the Quran at school, and could then attend a higher-level school called a *madrasa* and go on to study at university. Education had a religious basis, and produced scholars in a range of fields, from mathematics to poetry.

Al-Azhar University
Still a center of Sunni learning today, Cairo's al-Azhar University was founded by the Fatimid caliphate in the 10th century and became the world's most famous Islamic university. Renowned for its philosophical and theological scholarship, its name means "the resplendent."

Avicenna
The scholar Ibn Sina (980–1037), known in the West as Avicenna, wrote important books on medicine and philosophy, developing the work of the ancient Greeks.

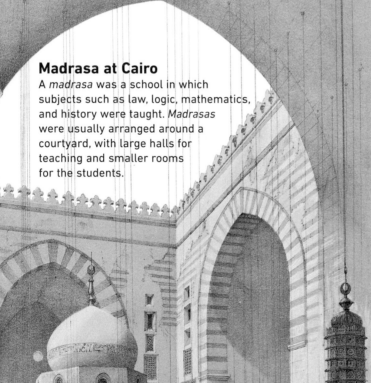

Madrasa at Cairo
A *madrasa* was a school in which subjects such as law, logic, mathematics, and history were taught. *Madrasas* were usually arranged around a courtyard, with large halls for teaching and smaller rooms for the students.

Globe
By the 13th century, Muslim scholars knew a vast amount about astronomy. They produced celestial globes like this to show the positions of stars in the sky.

Scholar's tomb
Sometimes a famous scholar was commemorated with a large tomb. Bin Ali, a notable scholar of the 14th century from Yemen, was buried in this striking double-domed tomb near Dhofar, Oman.

Library books

Centers of learning grew up in big cities such as Baghdad, Iraq, and Damascus, Syria, and had libraries that were often much larger than the collections in western cities and universities.

The Quran

Arabic scholarship has always been central to Islam. Muslims traditionally learn to recite the entire Quran by heart, and they always recite it in the original Arabic, whatever language they use in everyday life.

Law book

Muslim scholars produced some very advanced laws. From the earliest times, for example, Muslim women—unlike those in the West—had the right to own and inherit property. This book contains information about how inheritance was calculated.

Mullah

A mullah is a person who is learned in religion. Most mullahs have had a formal religious training, but the title can be given to someone with a reputation for religious scholarship.

Poetry reading

Recited or set to music, poetry was popular in Arabia even before the time of Muhammad, covering religion, love, and politics.

Calligrapher's inkpot

Inkpot of agate and gold

Calligraphy was an important and respected art. Its status is reflected in this very fine 19th-century inkpot.

Continued on next page

Writing

For Muslims, writing is one of the most important of all skills. Because Muslims believe that the Quran contains the words of Allah, scribes wish to reproduce those words correctly and with as much beauty as possible. Many Muslims, therefore, practice calligraphy, the art of beautiful writing. Calligraphy not only appears in books, it is also used to adorn buildings and other objects, providing decoration that carries a meaning.

Early scholars

This illustration from a 16th-century Persian text shows two children at Quranic school. Here they would receive the traditional education of young Muslims, learning to read, write, and recite the text of the Quran by heart.

Flowing maghribi script is one popular style of Islamic calligraphy.

Students at work

Some Muslim children, like these in Uzbekistan, still attend traditional Quranic schools. In many places, modern schooling has replaced this as the main type of education, although children may attend both kinds of school.

Fine calligraphy

Muslim calligraphers can make beautiful pictures using the curving forms of Arabic script. This horse is made up entirely of Arabic script, adorned with different colored inks.

Inscription written in legible form

Stone banners

Calligraphy appears on many Islamic buildings. At this *madrasa* in Konya, Turkey, bands of carved calligraphy curve around the doorway and cross in a knotlike form above it.

Pen and ink

Early calligraphers used pens made out of pieces of reed, cut to a point with a sharp knife. Black ink was made from soot, mixed with a little water to make it flow.

Animal-hair calligraphy brushes for larger characters

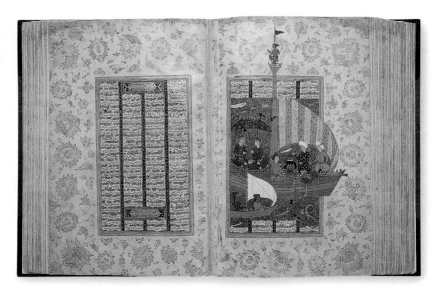

Inkwell
Bands of calligraphy decorate this dome-covered inkwell from 16th-century Iran. It would have inspired its user to produce writing of beauty and elegance.

Book of kings
This book is an epic poem from Iran, written in a flowing form of Arabic script called *nastaliq*. The long curves in the script are said to look like birds' wings.

Bookbinder
An Indian craftsman holds the pages of a book together to bind them. Bookbinding became an important craft because of the need to protect copies of the Quran.

Animal-hair calligraphy brushes for smaller characters

Broad-brush effects
Although a lot of calligraphy is done with pen and ink, an animal-hair brush is a useful tool for broad strokes and for filling in colors between black outlines. These brushes are made with goat and wolf hair.

Sindbad on his flying carpet, from The Arabian Nights

Arabian Nights
The Thousand and One Nights, or *Arabian Nights*, is a collection of magical stories said to have been told to King Shahryar by his wife Scheherazade. They still entertain readers today.

Spreading ideas

In a famous saying, Muslim scholars are told to "Seek knowledge, even unto China." During the Middle Ages, they led the world in many fields, from astronomy and mathematics to medicine and natural science. They gained much of their knowledge from the ancient world. Translating the works of ancient Greek scholars, they preserved information that had been lost or forgotten, and then built on this with their own work, carefully recording all their discoveries.

House of Wisdom
Under the Abbasids, the walled city of Baghdad in Iraq became an important center of learning, with its own university and numerous schools. The House of Wisdom, shown here, was built in the 9th century and was renowned among scholars for its huge library.

Horseshoe (or keyhole) arch in Cordoba, Andalusia, Spain

Architectural style
For centuries, Islamic architectural styles have varied from region to region, but simple exteriors often conceal lavish interiors decorated with geometric patterns and calligraphy. This sturdy but elegant horseshoe arch is typical of the Moorish style in North Africa and southern Spain.

Al-Idrisi map showing what was thought to be the shape of the known world in the 12th century

Africa

Arabia

Asia

Unlike modern western maps, south is at the top and north is at the bottom.

Europe

Al-Idrisi
Born in Morocco, writer and traveler al-Idrisi (1099–1180) worked for much of his life for the Norman king, Roger II of Sicily. He drew this map of the known world for the king and wrote a book on geography, describing the world north of the equator.

Shaft turned by donkey to operate scoop

Scoop raises water into a system of irrigation channels through fields.

Irrigation techniques
With water scarce in many parts of the Islamic world, inventors built irrigation devices. These ranged from simple systems, such as this donkey-powered water scoop, to a network of irrigation channels in Iran, built underground to reduce loss of water from evaporation—some are 12 miles (19 km) long.

Astronomy

The science of astronomy was important; it could be used to work out the direction of Mecca, so that people knew which way to face during prayers, and it helped determine the correct times to pray. Islamic astronomers developed better instruments, plotted precise tables showing the movements of the planets, and put together accurate calendars. Even the names of certain stars derive from Arabic words.

Jaipur observatory

This observatory at Jaipur, India, was built during the 18th century. Many of its instruments are built of stone—this great curving quadrant was used to measure the height of planets crossing the sky. Jaipur's astronomers drew on both Arab and earlier Indian science.

Istanbul observatory

In 1575, when the Ottoman Empire was at its height, astronomer Taqi ad-Din founded an observatory at Galata (now part of Istanbul, Turkey). This painting of the time shows the astronomers with their equipment, which includes a globe, a sand glass for timing, and all kinds of sighting devices.

Scales showing the positions of different stars

Central pivot

Rotating arm with pointer

Persian astrolabe

Astrolabe

The astrolabe is an instrument for measuring the height of a star or planet in the sky. It was probably invented by the ancient Greeks, but Muslim scholars and craft workers developed the instrument, making it more accurate and incorporating more data to show the positions of a host of different stars. It was especially useful to travelers, as it could help them to determine their position at sea.

Written instructions for using quadrant

Plumb line

Scale

Arabic quadrant

Quadrant

This instrument for measuring the height of a star consisted of a quarter-circle-shaped framework with a scale on the curving part of the frame and a plumb line hanging down vertically. The user looked at a star through a hole in the frame. The height of the star was shown at the point where the plumb line touched the scale.

Astronomy lesson

This group of scholars watches a teacher demonstrate an astrolabe. Observatories where lessons like this would have been held expanded rapidly in the 9th century, during the reign of Caliph Abdullah al-Mamun. The House of Wisdom he built in Baghdad, Iraq, had an observatory, and he ordered scientists there to produce more accurate astronomical tables.

Continued from previous page

Title page of the *Canon of Medicine*

Medicine

Early Islamic doctors knew a great deal about the diagnosis and treatment of diseases, anatomy, childcare, public health, and even psychiatry—and much of this knowledge is still relevant today. Medicine was also well taught, with students traveling thousands of miles to study at famous centers such as Baghdad's Adudi hospital.

Canon of medicine

The most famous book by scholar Ibn Sina is the *Canon of Medicine*. Ibn Sina based much of this book on the writings of ancient Greek physicians. A huge work, it covers subjects such as anatomy and hygiene, describes a vast range of diseases and injuries, and lists hundreds of different medicines.

The art of the pharmacist

The Islamic world produced the first specially trained pharmacists, who made their own medicines and worked closely with physicians. By the early 9th century, privately owned pharmacies were opening in Baghdad, where a flourishing trade with Asia and Africa provided a variety of medicinal herbs and spices.

Ivory handle decorated with a lion-head motif

Metal handle decorated with a ram's head

18th-century surgical knives

Under the knife

Spain's great 10th-century surgeon al-Zahrawi wrote about techniques such as treating wounds, setting bones, and removing arrows. He also designed many surgical instruments, and similar ones were used for hundreds of years.

Blade folds into handle for safety.

Scalpel

Scissors

Blood-letting

Like the ancient Greeks, Muslim physicians believed that bleeding a patient could cure many diseases. Although this practice seems crude today, the early Islamic doctors knew a great deal about blood and how it traveled around the body. One 13th-century Egyptian writer, Ibn an-Nafis, wrote about the circulation of blood some 400 years before it was "discovered" in Europe.

Folding handles

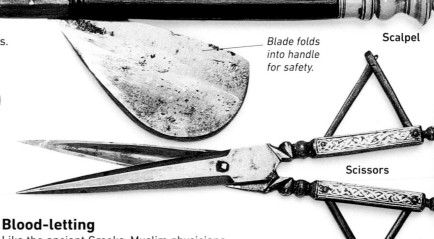

In storage

Many medicines were made with fresh herbs, but these could not always be found all year round. Herbalists therefore dried leaves, seeds, and other plant parts, so that they were available for use at any time of the year. Herbs were stored in glass or pottery jars, and these were usually sealed with a cork or stopper.

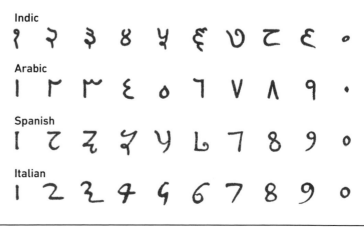

Dark color to keep out light

Pottery storage jars

Herbal medicine

The ancient Greek surgeon Dioscorides wrote a famous herbal encyclopedia that was translated into Arabic. Its five books describe all kinds of herbs, spices, roots, juices, and seeds that were used to make medicines and other preparations. This page from a 10th-century Arabic version of Dioscorides's book shows henna, a plant used widely in the Arab world as a dye.

Pointed blade for piercing and then cutting the skin

Vessel has rounded bottom to aid mixing.

Pestle and mortar

Well-prepared

Pharmacists and physicians often prepared medicines by grinding the ingredients together using a pestle and mortar. They made their preparations carefully, often following a standard textbook such as the 11th-century *al-Aqrabadhin,* which describes many different medications.

Mathematics

Modern mathematics was made possible by Islamic scholars. Mathematicians in Baghdad gathered ideas from ancient Greece and India, adding contributions of their own. They studied subjects such as calculation and geometry, and founded the science of algebra— a word that comes from the Arabic *al-jabr,* a term describing a method of solving equations.

Arabic numbers

The numbers we use today stem from 6th-century India, where place-value (giving a value to a number based on its place in a series of numbers) and the zero made calculation far easier than before. Taken up by Muslims, these ideas were probably passed to Europe in a 12th-century translation of an Arabic book on mathematics.

Indic

١ ٢ ३ ४ ५ ६ ७ ८ ९ ०

Arabic

١ ٢ ٣ ٤ ٥ ٦ ٧ ٨ ٩ ٠

Spanish

1 2 3 4 5 6 7 8 9 0

Italian

1 2 3 4 5 6 7 8 9 0

On the move

Both nomadic and settled peoples helped to spread Islam across western Asia and North Africa. Nomads moved from place to place in search of new grazing lands for their animals. Others lived in settlements, from small oasis villages to some of the world's most sophisticated cities, whose merchants took caravans of camels across the desert from one market to the next.

Oasis
Water trapped deep underground comes to the surface at oases, small patches of green among the desert's rock and sand. People can settle here and cultivate crops such as date palms. Oases are also vital water sources for nomadic desert peoples.

On the threshold
In nomadic and settled life alike, Islamic tradition sees the door as the meeting point between the private home and the public outside world.

Perched aloft
The people of Yemen were ideally placed because of the country's geographical position to make money from the water-borne trade in the Red Sea and build cities with beautiful tall brick houses like these. The comings and goings in such cities made Yemen a melting pot of ideas where both branches of Islam—Sunni and Shia— became well established.

Trading places
From Tangier in North Africa to Muscat in Arabia, most Muslim cities have always had markets that formed meeting places for traders all over the Islamic world—nomads, settled farmers, craft workers, and merchants from near and far. This coming together of peoples made markets prime places for the spread of Islam.

Wooden poles, supported by guy ropes, hold up the tent.

Rider and camel

Camels provide ideal desert transport—they can go for days without food or water, living off the fat in their humps. This one carries tasseled saddlebags. The rider's traditional Bedouin costume—a long white tunic covered by a sleeveless cloak, with a headcloth secured by two woolen coils—protects him from both sun and wind.

Flat, wide feet do not sink into the sand.

Clothing is woven from the wool of Bedouin camels, sheep, or goats.

Super saddle

Horses have always been important to the Arab people, especially the nomads, and Arabian horses are still widely prized today. This saddle is fit for the finest Arabian horse.

Nomadic Mongols

The Mongols of Central Asia, nomads who traditionally lived in round tents called yurts or gers, conquered Islamic lands in the 13th and 14th centuries, after which many Mongols became Muslims.

Bedouin tent

The Bedouins of Arabia and North Africa are desert-dwellers whose traditional life involves nomadic herding of camels, sheep, or goats. They were among the first to convert to Islam and spread the faith. Some Bedouin still live in long, low tents, though few are now nomads.

Islamic culture

Islam quickly developed its own style, which found unique expression in each of the diverse cultures that flourished within its empire. One famous *hadith* (Islamic saying) declares, "Allah is beautiful and loves beauty." Beauty was prized, and arts such as music, poetry, architecture, calligraphy, painting, textiles, metalwork, and ceramics were encouraged.

Fit for a sultan

The Topkapi Palace in Istanbul was home to the rulers of the Turkish Ottoman Empire from the 15th to the 19th centuries. Its richly decorated private apartments include the dining room of Sultan Ahmet III, adorned with colorful paintings of flower arrangements and bowls of fruit.

Decorated Quran

This copy of the Quran, made in the 17th century in Delhi, India, has patterns picked out in gold leaf. Not all copies are as richly decorated as this, but when copying the Quran, Muslim calligraphers always try to make their script as beautiful as possible.

Brushes

Ivory-handled knives

Bronze bird

This small statuette of a bird is an example of the metalwork of Persia and dates from the 12th or 13th century. The patterns on the bird's wing and body are typical of the period.

Writing box

Decorated with inlay and calligraphy, this writing box would have belonged to a very wealthy person. It contains pens, knives, brushes, inks, and other equipment for the calligrapher. The superb craftsmanship and luxurious materials of this object show the great importance placed on calligraphy in Islamic culture.

Patterned rug

The brightly colored patterns on this rug show how Islamic artists adapt shapes and other motifs from the natural world. The design is based on flowers, but they have been simplified, to give them a more abstract quality.

Sufis

Sufism is the name given today to the spiritual way at the heart of Islam. Its followers have their own spiritual practices and a distinctive culture of poetry and music. Sufis aim to find the inner meaning of Islam, and study under a spiritual teacher so as to come closer to Allah. Their practices may include ecstatic singing and sacred dance rituals that have earned one group of Sufis the nickname "whirling dervishes."

Tunic

The bold zigzag pattern on this tunic was made using a technique called *ikat*. This involves tie-dyeing the threads before weaving and is used widely in Central Asia.

Five double courses of strings

Lute

Arab music has its own instruments, and one of the most popular is the *oud*, the ancestor of the western lute. The *oud* is used for both solos and playing in a group of instruments. Its warm sound, and the subtle effects that skilled players can produce, have earned the instrument the title *amir al-tarab* (prince of enchantment).

Inlaid decoration

Pear-shaped body

Star tile

The beautiful ceramic tiles that decorate Islamic buildings usually have abstract or calligraphic patterns and can come in intricate shapes, like this star.

The Islamic city

Muslims inherited ideas about city planning from early civilizations and built large cities with far better facilities than Europe. A typical city in the year 1000 had a large mosque—usually with a school and library—a market, public baths, and caravanserais where traveling merchants could stay.

Town plan
Houses in an old Islamic city, such as Fez in Morocco, were tightly packed, but each had a private courtyard with a small garden and a fountain, as well as a flat rooftop. Many cities had public gardens beyond the walls.

Main mosque

City walls

Central square

Fountain
Public fountains, or *sabils*, are important in Islamic cities where the climate is often hot and dry. This square tower, known as the Sabil Kuttab of Katkhuda, is in Cairo, Egypt. Water for drinking or bathing is provided on the lower floor, while a school occupies the upper parts.

Market places
Suqs, or covered markets, are usually large, busy places. Shops selling similar goods are grouped close together so that purchasers can compare quality and prices, and so that the official market inspectors can do their job effectively.

Seeking a cure
Medicine was advanced in the Muslim world and some Islamic cities became renowned for their able doctors. Travelers would often return home with news of remarkable cures using remedies such as herbs and spices, and spread this knowledge further around the Islamic world and beyond.

Lookout tower gives a good vantage point and firing platform.

Battlements to conceal defenders.

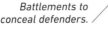

Public baths

Going to the baths was a social occasion—an opportunity to meet friends and exchange news—as well as a chance to get clean. This painting from Persia shows men visiting the baths. Women would use the baths at a different time of day.

Coffee houses

In some cities, comfortable coffee houses provided entertainment. People went to coffee houses, such as this one in Istanbul, Turkey, both for refreshments and to while away the hours listening to the local storyteller.

Pigeon post

Major Islamic cities were connected by a postal service using camels, mules, or horses. In 1150, the sultan of Baghdad even started a postal service using carrier pigeons.

City walls

The walls enclosing many Muslim cities had to be strong enough to keep out attackers, give somewhere for defenders to stand safely, and provide a good view of the surrounding countryside. Gates could be locked, to keep out enemies, but even when they were open, guards could keep an eye on who was entering and leaving the city.

City walls in Morocco

Waterwheel

This huge wooden waterwheel, mounted on a massive stone arch, was one of many built centuries ago in Hama, Syria, to raise water from the river to supply the town.

Trade and travel

When Muslim armies took over territory, traders were quick to follow, opening up routes that led east to China, south into Africa, northwest to Europe, and southeast across the Indian Ocean. The faith of Islam was soon spread by merchants as far as Malaysia and Indonesia. Muslims also traveled in search of knowledge, on diplomatic missions, and, of course, to make the hajj, or pilgrimage, to Mecca.

Ibn Battuta
Setting out on the hajj in 1325 from Tangier (in present-day Morocco), Ibn Battuta carried on, traveling 75,000 miles (120,000 km) in 29 years. He visited West and East Africa, Arabia, India, and China and, on his return, he described his adventures to the Sultan of Morocco.

Merchants on the move
This 13th-century illustration of merchants comes from a book by the writer al-Hariri, who came from Basra, Iraq. Men like these carried not only items for sale but ideas, inventions, and Islam itself.

Silver coins from Baghdad found in a Viking grave in Sweden

Coins for trade
Archaeologists have traced Islamic trade routes by unearthing Muslim coins as far afield as Scandinavia, Sri Lanka, and central China. Islamic coins were widely respected thanks to the high proportion of precious metals they contained, and greatly helped the growth of world trade.

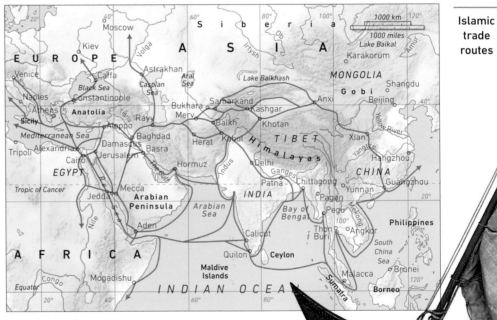

Islamic trade routes

Trade routes
Official reports, travelers' tales, and archaeology all provide clues about routes taken by Muslim traders. The Silk Road linked China and Europe, passing through many parts of the Muslim world on the way.

Salt caravan
This salt caravan is traveling to Timbuktu in Mali. Salt was essential for seasoning and preserving food and early Muslims sold it for vast sums. There were rich sources of salt in Africa, at places such as Taghaza (in present-day Algeria), where the locals even constructed buildings from salt. From here, caravans carried salt south, and the merchants spread Islam as they traveled.

Dhow

The most common trading vessels in the Indian Ocean were dhows, which are still used today. With their triangular sails, they are easy to maneuver and sail in headwinds. Their navigators studied the stars, often used the magnetic compass, and had an excellent knowledge of currents and winds.

Tasselled saddlebag

Camel

With their great staying power and their ability to produce milk on a diet of bitter vegetation and foul-tasting water, camels enabled the Muslims to survive and travel in inhospitable places. The two-humped Bactrian camel was used on northern routes, the one-humped dromedary in the south.

Ropes help support mast.

Furled lateen (triangular) sail

Main mast

Sweets on sale

For centuries, the Arab world has had a reputation for its sweets, and English words such as "sugar" and "candy" come from Arabic.

Nomad woman spinning

In this painting, the wife of an Egyptian herder is spinning wool to make thread. Some is used to make clothes for the family. What is left over can be sold at a local market.

Stern rudder

Continued on next page

Narwhal tusks

Among the marvels on sale in medieval markets were tusks taken from the narwhal, a small species of whale. Stories of the unicorn, the mythical beast with a single horn, fascinated people in the Middle Ages and unscrupulous traders claimed that narwhal tusks were unicorn horns.

Hunting birds

East and West, nobles enjoyed hunting with falcons. The Arab world bred some of the best, and most expensive, birds. Muslim envoys visiting the Chinese emperor during the Ming dynasty were asked to bring him falcons.

Frankincense

A resin from trees growing in southern Arabia, frankincense is burned for its perfume and was also used in medieval medicines. Burned as incense in Europe's churches, it became a major trade item for Muslim merchants.

Exotic goods

With extensive contacts over land and sea, Muslim merchants could trade in everything from African gold and Chinese porcelain to European amber and furs. They also brought back raw materials, which highly skilled craft workers then transformed into all kinds of items—leather goods, metalwork, textiles, glass—that were highly prized.

Cotton

Grown originally in Egypt and Iraq, cotton was a popular material for clothing because it was cool, comfortable, and cheaper than linen.

Cotton plant

Oils

Used in cooking, for soaps and cosmetics, and in lamps like this, oil was traded widely. The fine plant-based oils of the Muslim world were far more pleasant to use than the smelly fish oil that was often found in Europe.

Oil lamp

Camel caravan

Before modern forms of transport appeared, camel caravans, each beast loaded with bags containing trade goods, were a common sight in Arabia, the Sahara, and on the Silk Road across Asia.

Robe dyed using indigo

Colored dyes

Blue was a very popular color for fabrics and there was a valuable trade in indigo, a blue dye made from plants and used today in clothes such as denim jeans.

Silks

Muslim merchants brought silk yarns and finished fabrics from China along the Silk Road. The yarns were woven into cloth in cities such as Damascus, in Syria, and sold on to Western traders.

Silk fabric

Oyster shell with pearl

The ivory trade

Elephant ivory was brought across the Sahara and through Ethiopia to be exported from the ports of North Africa. Much of it went to Muslim Spain, where craft workers produced ivory objects such as intricately carved caskets.

Pearl fishing

Divers risked their lives in the fine pearl beds of the Arabian Gulf and Indian Ocean because of the huge demand in thriving pearl markets in Bahrain, Sri Lanka, and around the Strait of Hormuz, between Oman and Iran.

Pearl necklace

Elephant ivory

Food trade

The Muslim world developed a vigorous trade in various types of foods, and this business still continues today. Not only was there great financial gain for the merchants, but also western Europe was introduced to foodstuffs from all over Asia. Without Muslim merchants, Europeans would have had no rice, sugar, or coffee. In addition, the merchants set up trading colonies in many parts of the world, and this helped Islam to spread eastward as far as Southeast Asia.

Cinnamon sticks

Peppercorns

Ginger

Nutmeg

Cloves

Rice
When Muslims brought rice from Southeast Asia, it soon became a popular food in parts of Europe. Later, Western farmers learned how to grow rice for themselves.

Thai rice pot

The fruit trade
Muslims introduced new species of fruit, such as the apricot, into Europe. Dried fruit, such as dates, kept for a long time and could be carried for months. Fresh fruit did not travel so well, although highly valued melons were sometimes wrapped in lead to preserve them.

Cherries

Apricots

Figs

Dates

Precious spices
Grown on the islands of Indonesia, spices fetched high prices in Europe and western Asia, where they were used in food and medicines. Until the 16th century, Muslim merchants ran the spice trade, bringing nutmeg, cloves, cinnamon, and other spices to Arabia by sea and selling them at a huge profit to European traders.

Bedouin bag for coffee beans and cardamom pods

Sugar
An expensive luxury in the Middle Ages, sugar was brought west from Iran and Iraq to Muslim Spain. This enabled Muslim confectioners to create their own specialities—sherbet from Persia, various types of candy, sweets made from the licorice plant, and Turkish delight—all of which eventually reached Europe through trade.

Sherbet

Boiled sweets

Tea leaves

Green coffee beans

Tea and coffee
India and China were sources of tea, while coffee was grown in Yemen and traded from the town of Mocha. Both drinks became very fashionable in the West in the 18th century.

Turkish delight

Licorice

Sugared almonds

The Crusades

The city of Jerusalem is sacred to Islam, Christianity, and Judaism. From the 7th century, it was ruled by Muslims, who had mostly lived in harmony with the city's Christians and Jews. In the late 11th century, claiming the right to protect Christian pilgrims in the Holy Land, Europeans launched the Crusades—a series of largely unsuccessful wars to try to defeat the Muslims and take over Jerusalem and other nearby lands.

Preaching the Crusade
In 1095, Pope Urban II preached at Clermont, France. He called for a Christian army to capture Jerusalem. A number of European lords saw this as an opportunity to create power bases in and around the city.

Seljuk warriors
In the 11th century, Turkish warriors called the Seljuks, portrayed on this painted bowl, ruled a Muslim empire that stretched from Iran and Iraq to the eastern Mediterranean.

Engine of battle
The Crusades involved many sieges when the European armies attacked fortified cities such as Antioch and Damascus. They sometimes used powerful, outsized weapons such as this giant crossbow.

Winch for pulling back the bow string

Handle for aiming the crossbow

Bolt ready to fire

Into battle
In the First Crusade (1096–1099), several French and Norman knights, such as Godfrey of Bouillon, took armies to Jerusalem. After numerous battles with the Muslims, they were able to set up small kingdoms for themselves in the East.

Jerusalem
The First Crusade ended in July 1099 when Jerusalem fell to the Europeans, and Count Baldwin of Flanders was crowned king of the city. Christians remained in power here for more than 80 years.

Krak des Chevaliers

European crusaders who occupied the Holy Land built impressive castles as military bases. The mightiest of these was Krak des Chevaliers in Syria. It was rebuilt by French knights in the early 12th century, and its massive walls kept out any attackers.

Tall tower provides good lookout position.

Aqueduct for water supply

Wooden wheel

Richard "the Lionheart"

This English king was one of the leaders of the Third Crusade (1188–1192). He was a brave fighter and captured Acre, north of Jerusalem, after a two-year siege, but the crusade was badly organized and achieved little.

Illustration from a 13th-century French manuscript Historia Major

Saladin

Salah ad-Din, known in the West as Saladin, was a Muslim leader who fought a *jihad* (a struggle in accordance with strict limitations set by the Quran) against the crusaders under Richard the Lionheart. He retook Jerusalem in 1187.

Saladin's legacy

Saladin, who is buried in this tomb in Damascus, Syria, was a fearless fighter. He built up an empire in Syria, Palestine, and Egypt, and founded the Ayyubid dynasty, which ruled until 1260.

The Mamluks

Originally recruited to fight for the Muslims, Mamluks from the Caucasus region were not Arabs but became a military ruling class and defeated Christians in the later Crusades. After they had overthrown the Ayyubids in the 13th century, they ruled their own empire for more than 250 years.

Arms and armor

By the 11th century, Muslims were highly skilled in metal craftsmanship. The mounted warriors of the Islamic world used the sword, lance, and mace. Most were also skilled archers. Their finely made arms and armor were the envy of the non-Muslim world, but Muslim armies were also quick to adopt weapons that originated in the West, such as cannons and firearms.

Cannon miniature
European armorers were making cannons by the 14th century, and these powerful weapons were quickly taken up by Muslim armies—including these Ottomans at the Siege of Vienna in 1529.

Ottoman Turkish helmet
This helmet dates from around 1500. Made of iron and patterned with silver, it comes from the Turkish army's arsenal at Constantinople (now Istanbul).

19th-century Indian steel shield with gilt decoration

Shield of steel
The Mongols developed small, round shields made of leather—when the enemy's arrows got stuck in the leather, they could be pulled out and reused. Later round shields were made of steel, to protect the user from both sword blows and bullets. Shields like this were popular in India and Iran from the 18th century onward.

Sword and sheath of Shah Tamasp of Persia

Grenade
First used in China, grenades containing gunpowder were used by both Muslims and Christians in the Middle Ages. This 13th-century example from Damascus, Syria, was made of clay.

Handle hides a slender dagger.

Jambiya (and sheath, below right)

Mace
Carried as a sign of rank, maces were also fighting weapons used by mounted warriors and could break an opponent's bones, even if he was wearing armor.

Khanjar and decorated sheath

Steel mace from Persia

Shooting lesson
Hand-held guns first appeared in western Europe in the 15th century. Muslim craft workers soon started to make such weapons for themselves, often in workshops run by master-armorers from Portugal. In this picture, 16th-century Indian Emperor Akbar is learning how to handle one of the latest weapons.

Khanjar
In many parts of the Muslim world it was common for men, even boys, to carry weapons. This is a 20th-century dagger from Yemen, called a *khanjar*.

Jambiya
Originally from the Arabian Peninsula, the *jambiya* was a curved dagger that proved popular across the Muslim world as a plain fighting dagger or as an ornate ceremonial weapon.

Gold-barreled musket

Musket
When they were first imported to the East, guns like this European flintlock musket were resisted by high-ranking Muslim soldiers, who preferred the bow and the curved sword. But when their enemies began to take up firearms, Muslim warriors were forced to do the same, and weapons like the musket were valued all over Asia.

Swords and battle-axes
The tabar, or battle-ax, was a widespread weapon. Such axes had steel blades and were not always as ornate as this one, which is adorned with silver and gilding. Muslim soldiers also fought with distinctive swords with curved blades that broadened toward the tip. In Europe these were known as scimitars (above).

Spain

Moorish coin
The Moors—the name Christians gave to the Muslims from Morocco—brought with them their own coinage. After the defeat of the Moors, early Spanish Christian kings continued using Islamic designs on coins.

Muslims from Morocco invaded Spain early in the 8th century and ruled most of the Iberian Peninsula until the 15th century. In the 11th century, Moorish Spain began to be conquered by the Christian kings of the north and east, but southern cities such as Cordoba and Seville were centers of Islamic art and learning.

Great Mosque at Cordoba
Begun in the ninth century and later extended, Cordoba's Great Mosque, or Mezquita, was a symbol of Muslim power in Spain. It is a dazzling example of Islamic architecture. More than 850 columns of granite, jasper, and marble support a ceiling raised on double arches.

Minstrels
The musicians of Muslim Spain were among the best in Europe. Some were wandering minstrels who introduced European players to the lute and to using a bow to play stringed instruments.

The Alhambra, Granada
In the 14th century, Spain was ruled by the Nasrid dynasty who were based in Granada, southern Spain. Here they built the great fortified palace called the Alhambra, or "red palace," after the warm hue of its stone. It was designed to represent paradise on Earth and its tall towers and strong outer walls hide luxurious interiors.

Royal box
A great Moorish craftsman produced this ivory box during the 10th century. It was made for Al-Mughira, son of Abd al-Rahman III, the Umayyad caliph of Cordoba who reunited Spain after a period of disorder.

Scenes of courtly life

Alhambra courtyards

The beauty of the Alhambra lies not only in its exquisite Islamic decoration, but in the clever use of light and water to create a sense of space. Courtyards fill the palace with light, and many have tranquil pools that gently reflect the light. Arched walkways create shaded areas where the Nasrids could walk or relax.

Mudéjar tower

In many parts of Spain, Muslim craftsmen carried on working under Christian rule. They developed a style, now known as *mudéjar*, which used Islamic patterns to decorate brick-built wall surfaces, as in this tower at Teruel.

The last Muslim kingdom

As the Christians gradually conquered Spain, the Muslim rulers were pushed south. By the 15th century, only the kingdom of Granada in southern Spain remained in Muslim hands.

The gardens of the Generalife

The Quran describes paradise as a garden, watered by flowing streams. To escape from political life at the Alhambra, the Nasrid caliphs created a tranquil garden paradise on their country estate, the Generalife, which looked down over the city of Granada.

The last caliph

Boabdil became caliph in 1482, after a power struggle with his father that weakened Granada. In 1490, the Christian forces of Aragon and Castille laid siege to the city, which surrendered two years later. On his way to exile in Morocco, Boabdil looked back at the Alhambra and wept.

Moorish influence

This metalwork decorates a door in the royal palace in Seville. Built by a Spanish king, Pedro I, the palace shows the influence of Islamic art in Spain.

Africa

By the end of the Umayyad dynasty in 750, Islam had spread across North Africa from Egypt to Morocco. From here, it spread southward, as Muslim Berber and Tuareg merchants crossed Africa. While Muslims—mostly Sunnis—are in the majority in North and West Africa, and in many East African countries, Islam exists side by side with many different local cultures and political systems, from socialism to monarchy.

Woman warrior
One of the best known accounts of the Muslim conquests in North Africa is an epic called the *Sirat Bani Hilal*. One especially popular character is the heroine Jazia, a beautiful warrior who is shown here riding her camel.

Berber woman
The Berber peoples of the mountains and deserts of North Africa are Muslims and retain many of their local traditions, such as wearing bright-colored costumes and silver jewelry.

Wide margin allows the pages to be turned without touching the text.

Illuminated Quran
Calligraphy and other scholarly skills were as highly valued in Africa as in the rest of the Muslim world, and Africa had some famous centers of learning. One of the biggest of these was 15th- and 16th-century Timbuktu, in Mali. Scholars from all over North Africa came to the city's library to consult precious manuscripts, such as this copy of the Quran.

Earth pinnacle built around wooden post

Djenne mosque
Earth is the traditional building material in many parts of Africa—not only for houses, but for large buildings such as this mosque at Djenne in Mali. Djenne was one of the most important trading centers along the Niger River.

Sousse minaret
When the Muslim conquerors took over areas like Tunisia, they founded cities and built mosques in which to pray. The 9th-century mosque at Sousse, with its round stone minaret, is one early example.

Wearing the Quran

This tunic was worn by a warrior of the Asante people of West Africa. The pouches contain sacred texts to protect the warrior in battle.

Leather pouch holds a verse from the Quran.

Tile patterns

These hexagonal wall tiles from North Africa bear patterns of flowers, leaves, and twining stems made into abstract designs in typical Islamic style.

Precious metal

West Africa had fine gold workers before the arrival of Islam. The Muslims used these skills to produce gold coinage.

Memorizing the Quran

Islam brought formal education to many parts of Africa. This Mauritanian student is reading a *sura* (chapter) of the Quran, and learning it by heart.

A famous pilgrimage

Mali was the center of a large West African empire during the 14th century. Its ruler, Mansa Musa, made the pilgrimage to Mecca in 1324–1325 and his long journey is recorded on this map.

Smooth outer coating of mud protects walls.

Wooden beams strengthen the structure.

Domed tomb

Most Muslims have simple graves, with larger tombs for caliphs and other notable people. This tomb near Khartoum in Sudan, was probably built for a local saint. Its dome shows people can visit to pay their respects.

Mongols and Turks

In 1219, the lands of Islam were invaded by armies from Mongolia. By 1258, Mongols had sacked Baghdad and killed the caliph, devastating Islam's political center. Defeated by the Mamluks in 1260, many converted to Islam. The Turks founded the Ottoman Empire in 1290. In conquering much of eastern Europe, they became the dominant political force in Islam.

Genghis Khan
Mongol warlord Genghis Khan came to power in 1206 and launched a campaign of raiding and conquest. His empire stretched from China to the borders of Europe.

Mongol warrior
The Mongols were skilled horsemen and ruthless fighters. They killed millions and destroyed hundreds of settlements to bring much of Asia under Mongol rule.

Warrior bowl
The Mongols were proud of their warriors, as this decorated bowl from the 9th century shows. Originally a nomadic people, the Mongols had detailed knowledge of the land and were able to take their enemies by surprise.

Embroidered cloth

Pillar of skulls at Baghdad

The new Mongol capital
Genghis Khan's empire was divided between his sons and his grandson, Kublai Khan, who founded the Yuan dynasty in China. He built a new capital, which later became Beijing.

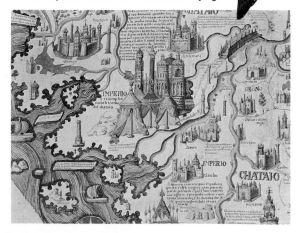

Ruthless Timur
The Turkish-Mongol leader Timur (known as Tamerlane in the West) claimed to be descended from Genghis Khan. This Muslim founder of the Timurid dynasty called himself "the Sword of Islam" and conquered much of the western Mongol Empire. When he took Baghdad in 1390, he put the skulls of his victims on display.

Fall of Constantinople

Constantinople (now Istanbul) was the capital of the Christian Byzantine Empire. During the Middle Ages, the Turks took over much of this empire. The city fell to the Sultan Mehmet II in 1453, and became the center of the Ottoman Empire.

Fortress of Rumeli Hisari, built by Mehmet II as a base from which to attack Constantinople

Recurved bow, the favorite Mongol weapon

Text reads: "Suleyman Shah son of Salim Shah Khan always triumphant."

Tughra of Suleyman I

Sign of the sultan

Each Ottoman sultan had a *tughra*, or official signature, specially created for him. It was designed to prevent forgery and could only be used by the sultan's staff. These staff were part of a huge civil service that the Ottomans developed for running their empire. Able civil servants could be promoted and rise to high social rank.

Suleyman the Magnificent

Suleyman I, known in the West as "the Magnificent" and in the East as "the Lawgiver," ruled from 1520 to 1566, when the Ottoman Empire was at its height. Determined to extend the empire, he advanced into Europe and, in 1529, he besieged Vienna, in Austria. Despite his powerful army, he failed to capture the city.

The Conqueror

Ottoman sultan Mehmet II was known as "the Conqueror" after his capture of Constantinople in 1453. Interested in all types of culture, he attracted scholars and craftsmen from all over the Muslim world to his court and had his portrait painted by the Italian artist Bellini.

51

Burning bright

The Ghaznavids, whose craftsmen made this metalwork lamp, were Seljuk rulers who controlled Afghanistan and much of Iran and were at the height of their power in the early 11th century. As Sunni Muslims, they opposed the rival Shia dynasty, the Buyids, in Iran.

Pierced decoration

Lamp is made of cast bronze.

Central Asia, Iran, and India

Islam came early to Iran, which was conquered by Muslim rulers by the year 641. A series of dynasties followed, including the Seljuks from Turkey, the Mongols from Central Asia, the Timurids, and the Safavids. Muslims also ruled all or part of India from 1193 to the 19th century, when the subcontinent became part of the vast British Empire. After India won independence in 1947, the new Muslim state of Pakistan was born.

Timur's tomb

The Mongol war leader Timur (Tamerlane) had victories in Iran, India, Syria, and Turkey. When he died in 1405, he was trying to overrun China, too. The vast wealth he amassed from his military conquests is reflected by the rich decorations of his tomb at Samarkand in Central Asia.

Isfahan

Isfahan, Iran, was the capital of the Safavid dynasty (1501–1732), which unified the area and made Shia Islam the state religion. The Safavid sultans added many fine buildings to the city, including a large palace complex, and enhanced the Great Mosque (left). The red-and-blue glazed tilework of the 16th–17th centuries is in typical Safavid style.

Qutb Minar, Delhi

In 1193, Afghan ruler Muhammad al-Ghuri conquered northern India. He built a capital at Delhi from which Muslim sultans ruled, putting up buildings such as this tall minaret. The Delhi sultanate ended in 1526.

Khwaju Bridge

Built by the Safavids, the Khwaju Bridge in Isfahan, Iran, is about 440 ft (133 m) long and spans the Zayandeh River with 23 arches. This river crossing also acted as a dam to irrigate nearby gardens.

The Mughal Empire

The Muslim Mughal dynasty ruled in India from 1526 to 1858. Under early Mughal emperors, the diverse Indian subcontinent was united and underwent a unique period of achievement in art, music, literature, and architecture. Under the later Mughal rulers, however, the empire began to fall apart.

Akbar leads his army into battle.

Babur discusses building progress with his architects.

Babur

The first Mughal emperor was Babur, who came from Iran and was descended from Timur and Genghis Khan. The word Mughal comes from "Mongol," because of Babur's origins. Babur was just 11 when he became a ruler in Transoxiana, and conquered Samarkand at the age of 14. He established a kingdom in Iran, which he lost, and another in Afghanistan. In 1526, Babur conquered India. A well-educated man, he was a poet and historian who encouraged the arts.

Akbar

The greatest Mughal emperor was Akbar, who ruled from 1556 to 1605. He set up an efficient bureaucracy, whose structure still influences Indian government today. As one of the most tolerant rulers, he abolished a tax on his Hindu subjects, and encouraged artists to combine Hindu and Islamic styles in their work.

Aurangzeb

This book contains the letters of the emperor Aurangzeb (1658–1707). He expanded the empire, but weakened it by failing to invest in agriculture and support his army or his court. He also persecuted non-Muslims, taxing Hindus heavily and destroying many of their temples.

The Far East

Arab traders brought Islam to coastal cities in China during the 7th century, but only in the extreme west of China, settled by people of Mongol descent, did sizeable Islamic populations develop. Islam also reached Southeast Asia through trade, and today the largest Muslim population in the world is in Indonesia.

Name of Allah

Outline of bird where wax covered the fabric during dyeing

By sea
Some Muslim merchants traveled from the mainland to Southeast Asia in traditional boats with curved prows.

Typical Chinese upward–curving roof

Batik
China and Southeast Asia have always traded in beautiful fabrics, such as silks. This piece has been dyed using the process called batik, which was invented in Java. The dyer applies wax to the parts of the fabric which are to remain uncolored, then soaks the material in dye. When dry, the material is boiled or scraped to remove the wax.

Carved stone motif at Xian mosque

Great Mosque of Medan
Built in the early 20th century, the Great Mosque of Medan in Sumatra, Indonesia, is a superb example of Islamic art and architecture, and a popular pilgrim site. Materials include marble and stained glass from France, Germany, and Italy.

Grand Mosque of Xian
During China's Cultural Revolution (1966–1976), all religions were outlawed, and mosques were destroyed or closed. In the 1980s, many mosques were reopened or rebuilt. China's oldest mosque, the Grand Mosque in Xian, can be visited today.

Rod puppet

The shadow puppet theatre called *wayang golek* is performed with carved and painted wooden figures that are manipulated with rods. *Wayang* is a traditional Javanese entertainment, widely enjoyed by Muslims at festivals and celebrations.

Articulated arm

Wooden rod is used to move puppet's arm.

Clothing conceals stick used to hold puppet.

Wearing the *tudong*

These schoolgirls from Brunei are wearing the *tudong*, a form of head-covering that extends down to conceal the neck and upper body. Wearing the *tudong* is just one way in which women can obey the Quran's instruction to dress modestly.

Rice bowl

Rice is the staple food in both China and Southeast Asia. It is eaten from small round bowls made of porcelain—a type of pottery that was widely traded, forging an important link between China, the Muslim world, and the West.

Caravanserai

Merchants traveling by land needed places to stay, so the locals built caravanserais on the routes through Asia to China. In these simple stone buildings, merchants could find a bed and somewhere to stable their camels.

Mix of styles

This modern mosque in Kuala Kangsar, Malaysia, was built after the country became independent in 1957, when Islam was recognized as the state's official religion.

Malaysian mosque

A magnet for trade, Southeast Asia has been influenced by many cultures. This Malaysian mosque is decorated in the style of those in Iran and India.

Costume and jewelry

The Quran instructs women and men to dress modestly, but Muslims wear all sorts of different clothes, including modern western dress. Traditional garments are often worn for special occasions such as family celebrations.

The *hijab*
Many Muslim women wear the traditional Islamic headscarf, or *hijab*, which covers the head, hair, and neck. The scarves come in many colors and can be tied in various ways to look both stylish and modest.

Uzbek bride
In many places, wedding celebrations are a time to put on elaborate traditional costumes. This bride from Uzbekistan wears a gold headdress, a dress of rich fabrics woven with gold threads, and a long, embroidered head-covering.

Coin robe
In Arabia and western Asia it is an old custom to wear much of your wealth. This Bedouin robe has coins stitched to it. It is made of natural cotton, which is comfortable to wear in the desert heat.

Saudi Arabian woman wearing a face veil

The veil
In some Muslim communities, it is customary for women to veil their faces. The veil may cover the lower part of the face, up to the eyes, or the whole face, as here.

A new twist
Muslim boys often wear this type of brightly colored cap. The shape is traditional, as is the technique of embroidery, but these helicopters are modern.

Gold bracelet
For centuries, Arab metalworkers worked mostly in silver, but now gold is a popular material for jewelry that is bought for a bride when she marries.

Head decoration
This is a traditional form of jewelry in the Arabian Peninsula. A woman wears a pair of head decorations, one over each ear.

Chains and roundels made of silver

Amulets
Some Muslims wear an amulet—a small ornament or piece of jewelry with Quranic texts to protect them from evil.

Enameled necklace
Jewelry can be given bright red, blue, and green colors by enameling. This involves applying a mixture of powdered colored glass to the metalwork and heating the piece in a kiln to make the decoration hard and permanent.

Two-way pattern
The outside of this robe from Central Asia was produced using the centuries-old art of *ikat* that was passed down through the generations by master dyers and weavers of handspun silk. The lining stands out as its flower patterns contrast well with the zigzag *ikat*.

Dazzling design
This North African robe shows two forms of bright, colorful decoration. The stripes are made by sewing different colored fabrics together. But what really makes the robe stand out is the encrustation of brilliantly colored beads.

Islamic society

The Quran tells Muslims that man is God's vice-regent on Earth and is responsible for taking good care of everything, from the environment to the people around him. Muslims are told to be tolerant of other peoples and to create societies in which justice, kindness, and the avoidance of wrongdoing are upheld—virtues which start within the family.

Sultan and subjects
Muslim countries are governed in different ways. In the past, many had heads of state who ruled with absolute power, like this Moroccan sultan. After World War I, the Ottoman Empire was dissolved, the last caliphate was abolished in 1924, and most Muslims now live in modern nation states.

Selling slaves
Slavery was common during the time of Muhammad and long after, as this medieval picture of a slave market shows. The Quran encouraged the freeing of slaves and insisted they be treated with kindness.

Scales of justice
Known as *sharia*, Islamic law demands ethical conduct in all areas of life, including business. Since Abbasid times, markets in Muslim countries had officials who checked weights and measures and the quality of merchandise.

"Allah created nothing finer on Earth than justice. Justice is Allah's balance on Earth, and any man who upholds this balance will be carried by Him to Paradise."

THE PROPHET MUHAMMAD

Tolerance
The Quran stresses tolerance between Muslims and non-Muslims. Jews and Christians are given particular respect—since they, too, believe in the One God—and should be able to coexist peacefully, like the Muslim and Christian chess-players in this Spanish picture.

Marching together
Many Muslims live side by side with people of very different beliefs. For the most part, they live in harmony, like these Muslims and Buddhists in China.

Spires and minarets
In Zanzibar, Tanzania, the mosque and the Christian church are close neighbors. Here, as in many places, Muslims live in a diverse community, side by side with Christians and those who follow other religions.

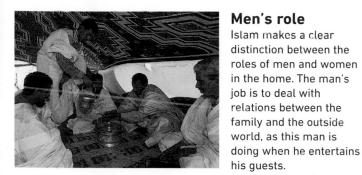

Men's role
Islam makes a clear distinction between the roles of men and women in the home. The man's job is to deal with relations between the family and the outside world, as this man is doing when he entertains his guests.

Children and family
Muslims regard children as gifts of Allah and a great joy in life. Parents are expected to care for their children and to give them a good upbringing and education. Children are expected to respect and obey their parents and be conscientious, virtuous, and kind toward them.

Henna for the bride
Henna is used in a traditional ritual that is usually performed on the day before a marriage. The bride's hands and feet are adorned with beautiful patterns using a dye made from henna leaves. This may be done by the bride's female friends and relatives.

Married life
Muslims are usually expected to marry and have children. Marriage brings the couple, their families, and the community together, reflecting the harmony of Allah's creation.

Dowry
A Muslim man gives his bride-to-be a dowry, a payment in money or property, which may be presented in a box like this.

Pattern is said to symbolize strength and love.

Sports
A growing number of Muslim women are taking part in sports and many are proud to wear the hijab when playing and competing. Here, a student and her coach at an Islamic college in Australia are practicing soccer skills.

Women's work
In traditional Muslim societies such as Sudan, women usually keep to their roles of home-making and childcare. But in many societies, Muslim women are educated to a high level, work in professions such as medicine and law, and take a prominent part in public life.

Local terra-cotta pot

Man at prayer
In Islam, all comes from Allah and will eventually return to Allah. Qualities that are loved in family, friends, and wider society come from Allah. So the individual's relationship with Allah is paramount. Each Muslim turns to Allah for guidance, forgiveness, and support.

Festivals

Yearly festivals in the Muslim calendar mark key events in the history and practice of the faith, such as the Prophet's birthday and the Five Pillars of Islam: Eid al-Adha (the feast of the sacrifice) occurs during the time of the hajj, and Eid al-Fitr at the end of Ramadan. From birth to marriage, key points in a Muslim's life are also celebrated.

Lunar calendar
The Islamic calendar is based on the phases of the moon. Each year has 12 lunar months of 29 or 30 days each, and a total of 354 or 355 days. Each month begins with the sighting of the new moon.

Ramadan
During the month of Ramadan, Muslims fast between sunrise and sunset, then pray and eat. Special lights like this one may be lit during the evening meal.

Kerbala
Kerbala, Iraq, is where Muhammad's grandson Husayn was killed in 680. Husayn's shrine is sacred to the Shia Muslims. His death is marked by the festival of *Ashura* (see opposite).

Mawlid an-Nabi
These boys from Kenya are taking part in a procession celebrating Mawlid an-Nabi, the birthday of the Prophet. This day is a public holiday and is also marked with recitations of a poem called the *Burdah*, in praise of Muhammad.

"Eid Mubarak"
During the festival of Eid al-Fitr, people greet neighbors with the phrase "Eid Mubarak" (Blessed Eid), and send Eid greeting cards (left).

Eid greeting card

Stained glass panel

Eid balloons
Colorful balloons abound during Eid al-Fitr, which marks the end of Ramadan. Celebrations include a festival prayer, a hearty breakfast, and the giving of alms to the poor.

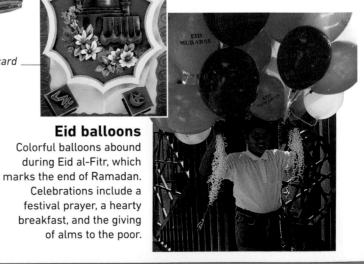

The Islamic calendar

Muharram	Safar	Rabi al-Awwal
The sacred month, 30 days—1: *Al-Hijra* (New Year) 10: *Ashura*	The month which is void, 29 days.	The first spring, 30 days—12: Mawlid an-Nabi (birthday of the Prophet)

Sallah festival

Some Muslim festivals are local celebrations unique to one country or region. The Durbar or *Sallah* festival is held in northern Nigeria as part of the rituals marking the end of Ramadan. The highlight is a procession that features chiefs in ceremonial robes, brightly costumed horsemen, and lute players.

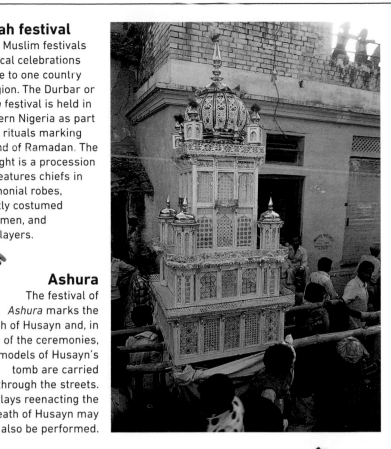

Ashura

The festival of *Ashura* marks the death of Husayn and, in one of the ceremonies, models of Husayn's tomb are carried through the streets. Plays reenacting the death of Husayn may also be performed.

Whirling dervish

Members of the Sufi Mevlevi order hold festivals at which they perform their "whirling" dance, known as *sama'*. One such festival marks the death of their founder, the great Sufi poet and mystic, Jalaluddin Rumi (1207–1273).

Wedding celebrations

In Islam, a contract of marriage is made by the groom giving the bride-to-be a dowry, and by the bride then giving her consent to marriage before witnesses. Wedding celebrations vary according to the local traditions, but will usually include recitations from the Quran and a great feast.

Dowry purse

Khitan

Muslim boys are usually circumcised in a ceremony called *khitan*. This is often done around age 7, though it may be done any time before a boy reaches 12 years old. These Turkish boys are attending a mosque before their *khitan* ceremony.

Laylat al-Miraj

On the 27th day of the month of *Rajab*, Muslims celebrate Muhammad's Night Journey and his Ascension to Heaven. This is called *Laylat al-Isra w'al-miraj*, the Night of the Journey and Ascension.

Buraq, the miraculous steed that carried the Prophet on his Night Journey

Rabi al-Thani	**Jumada al-Ula**	**Jumada al-Thani**
The second spring, 29 days	The first month of dryness, 30 days	The second month of dryness, 29 days

Continued on next page **61**

Food

A rich variety of food originated in the Islamic countries, and many of these foods have spread far and wide. This variety is only slightly limited by some simple dietary rules that restrict what a Muslim may eat. Islam forbids the drinking of alcohol, and Muslims are not allowed to eat pork which, as in other traditions, is considered to be unclean. Other animals may be eaten, provided that they are slaughtered in the correct way, with the Name of God pronounced as the creature's life is taken. Meat that is slaughtered in this way is described as halal, or lawful to eat.

Sweet tray
With access to sugar, many Muslim areas have developed their own traditional types of sweets. Those pictured come from Malaysia. Known as *kuch*, they are rich cakes flavored with palm sugar and coconut.

Mint tea
Tea is widely drunk in many Muslim countries. Usually served in a glass, hot, sweet mint tea is very popular and refreshing. Lemon tea is a common alternative.

Cardamom **Cumin**

Turmeric

Spices
The spice trade was always important to Muslim merchants, so many spices from India and Southeast Asia found their way into the cooking of the Middle East. Ingredients such as cumin and cardamom were valued for their fragrance and flavor, and as aids to digestion.

On sale
This mother and daughter in Isfahan, Iran, are buying food from a local dealer in dried fruit and spices. In this traditional shop, most of the goods are displayed loose, so that purchasers can see exactly what they are buying.

Fast food
Street sellers cooking and selling their own food are a common sight in the Islamic world. In Egypt, street vendors like this man sell passersby falafel cooked in the open air and flavored with local herbs.

Date palm
Date palms are grown all over the dry areas of western Asia and northern Africa, and dates are a popular staple food.

Rajab	**Shaban**	**Ramadan**
The revered month, 30 days— 27: *Laylat al-Miraj* (Night Journey)	The month of division, 29 days—15: *Laylat al-Barat* (memory of the dead, Iran and India)	Month of great heat, 30 days—27: *Laylat al-Qadr* (Night of the Descent of the Quran)

For the sweet tooth

Sweet pastries are one of the delights of western Asia. This shop in Syria is selling local pastries called *hama*, which get their sweetness from a covering of honey. Several varieties are displayed in the shop window to tempt passersby.

Bread-maker

Unleavened bread—bread baked without yeast, so that it stays flat—is a common staple food throughout the Islamic world. This woman in Kyrgyzstan is making it on an open fire, but it may also be baked on a hot stone.

Oranges

Brought to Europe along trade routes from the Islamic world, oranges were quenching western thirsts by about the 14th century. The very term orange is derived from the Arabic word *naranj*.

Lamb kebabs

Grilling small pieces of meat on a skewer to make a tasty kebab is common in the eastern Mediterranean and Turkey. Kebabs made with minced lamb, cubes of lamb, or pieces of chicken, are popular across Europe and beyond.

Sharing a meal

Hospitality has always been a virtue in Islam, especially in the desert, where food is hard to come by. This early illustration shows some Persians sharing food with a stranger.

Coffee pot

Another item introduced to the West by the Muslims is coffee. Excellent coffee has been grown for centuries in the south-western corner of the Arabian Peninsula. It is still served there today, usually very strong and sweet, from elegant pots like this.

Family food

This family in Senegal is cooking their meal over an open fire, and will all eat out of the one pot. This daily family gathering is a chance to catch up on the news, as well as enjoy a welcome meal together.

Shawwal	**Dhu al-Qidah**	**Dhu al-Hijjah**
The month of hunting, 29 days—1: Eid al-Fitr (Feast of Fast-breaking)	The month of rest, 30 days	Month of the Pilgrimage, 29 or 30 days—10: Eid al-Adha (Feast of Sacrifice)

Did you know?

☪★ Chess was likely invented in India, but the first known mention of the game is in an ancient Islamic poem. By the 8th century, it was so popular in Persia that chess championships were held in the caliph's palace.

☪★ "Tales of Sindbad the Sailor," "Ali Baba and the Forty Thieves," and "Aladdin and His Magic Lantern" all originated in *The Arabian Nights*, a collection of Islamic stories that dates to the 9th century.

Sindbad carried by an eagle

Illustration from *The Arabian Nights*

☪★ The trade and cultivation of coffee originated in the Islamic world. Coffee beans were traded from the town of Mocha, which has given its name to a strong, rich brew. People drank coffee not only at home but also in coffee houses, where they could chat, listen to music, or catch up with the day's news.

☪★ The Chinese showed their Islamic trading partners how to make paper, but Muslims used linen rather than mulberry bark as the raw material, which led to better paper. Islamic paper was regarded as the finest in the world.

Muslims praying after a Ramadan meal

☪★ How did ancient Muslim farmers get water in a desert? Through *qanats*, an underground network of tunnels linked to a series of manholes. These tunnels, completely dug by hand, carried water from an aquifer to outlying areas. There are around 22,000 *qanats* in Iran, covering 170,000 miles (273,588 km). Remarkably, most of them are still in use, even though they are thousands of years old.

☪★ The Islamic skill in calligraphy means that many books are works of art. In fact, a great calligrapher is given the same acclaim as a painter and sculptor might receive in the West. The artistry of Islamic illumination, miniature painting, and bookbinding is also greatly prized.

Pen-and-ink calligraphy

Early Islamic book

☪★ Once paper was made, Muslim traders developed a paper-based economy. The ancient Persian word for an order for payment, *saak*, is the origin of our word "check."

☪★ The minaret of La Giralda in Seville, Spain, built by Islamic architects in the 12th century, may have been Europe's first observatory, used by astronomers to map the heavenly bodies.

Backgammon is still a popular game in Muslim countries.

☪★ Backgammon is an ancient board game, first played 5,000 years ago in Mesopotamia. Players used stones as markers and dice made of stones, bones, wood, or clay on a wooden playing board.

☪★ Algebra, the equation-based branch of mathematics, gets its name from the Islamic word *al-jabr*, which means "completion." A Muslim mathematician wrote the first known algebra book in the 11th century.

☪★ Windmills were used in Persia as early as the 7th century BCE. They did not appear in Europe until the 12th century, after crusaders had come into contact with Muslims.

☪★ Legend has it that Muhammad cut off one of his sleeves when it was time to go to prayer rather than disturb his cat, who was napping on it. The distinctive "M" on a tabby cat's forehead is said to be a lasting sign of Muhammad's affection for cats.

☪★ Paris, France, has the largest Muslim population of any city outside the Islamic world. The Detroit suburb of Dearborn, Michigan, has the largest Muslim population in the US.

QUESTIONS AND ANSWERS

Q Is Islam the oldest of the world's major religions?

A No. It is the youngest of the three great monotheistic (the belief that there is only one God) religions—Judaism and Christianity are older.

Q How large is the world's Muslim population?

A Latest estimates put the number of people who follow Islam at 1.8 billion—about one in four people on the planet. Christianity is the largest religion, but Islam is the fastest-growing faith.

Q Which nation has the largest Muslim population?

A There are some 200 million Muslims in Indonesia. This represents about 85 percent of the country's total population.

Q How many Muslims live in the United States?

A It is difficult to estimate the number of American Muslims. The US Constitution prohibits questions about religion in the census, but a study published in 2016 estimates that there are 3.3 million Muslims living in the US, which is about 1 percent of its total population.

Q What is the difference between "Islam" and "Muslim"?

A "Islam" is the name for the religion itself, and "Muslim" is the name for a follower of Islam. It is the same thing as the difference between Christianity and a Christian.

Q Where is the spiritual center of Islam?

A The spiritual heart of the Muslim world is in the Haram, the sacred enclosure in Mecca, the birthplace of the Prophet Muhammad in Saudi Arabia.

Q Who was Muhammad?

A Tradition has it that Muhammad was born in 570 and belonged to the Quraysh tribe. Orphaned as a boy, he was brought up by his grandfather and uncle and worked as a merchant before becoming the Prophet of Islam.

Thousands of pilgrims gather at Mecca

Q What is the Quran? Is it the same as the Koran?

A The Quran (often spelled Koran) is the holy book of Islam containing the word of God, as revealed to the Prophet.

A 1,200-year-old Quran

Q When was the Quran first written down?

A The Quran was written down soon after Muhammad's death, by scribes under Uthman, the third caliph.

Q Do all Muslims practice the same form of Islam?

A Not quite. About 90 percent of Muslims are Sunnis, who follow the teachings of Muhammad. The other 10 percent are Shias, who also follow the teachings of his descendants. They have developed different devotions and practices, but both groups essentially practice the same religion.

Q What is a mosque?

A The place where Muslims gather to pray and worship. A tower called a minaret is a common feature to all mosques. Inside the mosque there is a *mihrab*, a decorated niche in the wall that marks the direction of Mecca. The *minbar* is a pulpit to the right of the *mihrab*, and there is a large, open area for people to pray in.

Q Who leads the prayer at a mosque?

A The imam leads the prayers and teaches people at a mosque. Religious authority rests with the Quran, not with a person. There are no priests, as there are no sacraments. Every Muslim is his own "leader" because he or she must carry out the Five Pillars, the obligations of the religion.

Record breakers

☾★ **LARGEST MOSQUE**
The enormous Shah Fiesal mosque (below) in Islamabad, Pakistan, can hold 100,000 people.

☾★ **TALLEST MINARET**
The minaret at Shah Alum, Selangor, near Kuala Lumpur, Malaysia, is 450 ft (137 m) tall.

☾★ **OLDEST STANDING MINARET**
The minaret at the mosque in Kairouan, Tunisia, was built in 728 CE.

☾★ **OLDEST MOSQUE**
The Ummayed Mosque in Damascus, Syria, is thought to be the world's oldest mosque, completed in 705 CE.

Find out more

Islam is often in the news, but to learn more about its faith, history, and traditions, start with your local mosque or Islamic center. They function as information centers for the local Muslim community, so you will be able to find out about special events in your area. Visit your local library, too, for more books on Islam, and look online to find the nearest museum with a collection of Islamic art, from tiles to textiles.

Visit a museum's Islamic collection

Because of the prohibition of the depiction of humans and animals, Islamic art developed its own distinctive traditions. Pay a visit to the Islamic hall of an art museum, such as the V&A in London or the Los Angeles County Museum of Art (above), to see superb examples of Islamic painting, architecture, books, and decorative arts.

Islamic art

This beautiful star-shaped tile creates an immediate impact with its strong color and interesting design. Because so many mosques are tiled inside and out, tile-making is a highly developed art in the Muslim world.

Abstract design

Calligraphy

Pens like these were used to create Islamic calligraphy. If you would like to try your hand at this ancient art, check with your local art museum or look online for nearby classes.

Stylized decoration based on geometric and floral designs

USEFUL WEBSITES

- A site for non-Muslims who want to understand Islam: **www.islamicweb.com**

- A portal to information on Islam and the Muslim community: **www.islamicfinder.org**

- An independent, multi-faith online community: **www.beliefnet.com**

- Explore Muslim heritage through picture galleries, videos, and feature articles: **www.muslimheritage.com**

- Hear how each letter in the Arabic alphabet is pronounced: **http://abcsofarabic.tripod.com/alphabetpage.htm**

- A site to help put today's news from the Middle East into perspective: **www.pbs.org/wgbh/globalconnections/mideast/index.html**

- Companion site to PBS Frontline documentary on Muslims: **https://www.pbs.org/wgbh/pages/frontline/shows/muslims/**

- Activities for young children learning about the pilgrimage to Mecca: **http://www.muslimkidsguide.com/10-ways-children-can-have-fun-learning-about-hajj/**

Inside a mosque

All mosques contain a *mihrab*, a niche in the wall that shows the direction of Mecca. This horseshoe-shaped arch over a *mihrab* in Cordoba, Spain, is richly decorated and a beautiful example of Islamic architectural style.

Islamic culture

Ask at your local Islamic center or check the Internet or newspaper listings for Islamic festivals or cultural events in your area. You might learn to write your name in calligraphy, hear traditional music, try different foods, or see a dance performance. These dancers in Croatia are performing the traditional Moreska dance. Dating as far back as 1156, it tells the story of a Muslim and Christian encounter during the age of the Crusades.

New York's Brooklyn Bridge

Muslim neighbors

Islam is the world's second-largest religion, after Christianity, and its 1.8 billion followers make up approximately 24 percent of the global population. It is also the fastest-growing religious group in the world. All the more reason to find out more about Islam, no matter where you live. Ask what your school or family knows about Islam in your neighborhood.

Islam in the movies

Muslims may be misrepresented in movies, but Spike Lee's *Malcolm X* is a more balanced view of the civil rights leader and his conversion to Islam.

Cultural centers

The Islamic Cultural Center in Washington, D.C., is the largest mosque in the United States. Although non-Muslims may not attend prayers, the mosque and its library welcome visitors at other times. If you plan to visit a mosque or Islamic center, remember to check the visiting times and dress code before you go, and always show respect in a place of worship.

PLACES TO VISIT

ALHAMBRA, GRANADA
To see Moorish architecture at its finest, visit the palace complex, Patio of the Lions, gardens, and museums—or take a virtual tour at www.alhambradegranada.org.

LOS ANGELES COUNTY MUSEUM OF ART, CA
The museum's permanent collection features Islamic art dating back to the 7th century.

ARTHUR M. SACKLER MUSEUM, HARVARD UNIVERSITY, CAMBRIDGE, MA
This collection of 2,500 works features pottery, textiles, and lacquers, and has a large number of Islamic paintings.

METROPOLITAN MUSEUM OF ART, NEW YORK
One of the most comprehensive collections of Islamic art, it contains nearly 12,000 objects from as far west as Spain and Morocco and as far east as India and Central Asia.

DETROIT INSTITUTE OF ARTS, MICHIGAN
This collection of Islamic decorative art is especially strong in the art of the book.

VICTORIA AND ALBERT MUSEUM, LONDON
The Jameel Gallery displays a dazzling selection from the V&A's extensive holdings of Islamic ceramics, glass, woodwork, weaponry, and textiles—including one of the world's oldest and largest carpets.

Message from the Quran on a mosque wall

Glossary

ADHAN The call to prayer; often made by a *muezzin*.

ALGEBRA A mathematical system in which letters or other symbols are used to stand for numbers.

AL-MASJID AL-HARAM MOSQUE The Sacred Mosque in Mecca, Saudi Arabia; Islam's holiest site, also known as the Great Mosque, it is the center of the annual hajj (pilgrimage), and is the world's largest mosque.

ALLAH The name of the one God in whom Muslims believe and upon whom all life and all existence depends.

ALMSGIVING The giving of gifts to the poor and needy; one form of almsgiving, *zakat*, is one of the Five Pillars of Islam.

ARABIA A peninsula in southwest Asia between the Red Sea and Persian Gulf.

ARABS Semitic people originally from the Arabian Peninsula, now living across southwest Asia and North Africa.

ASR The late afternoon prayer.

ASTROLABE An instrument once used to find the altitude of a star or other heavenly body.

ASTRONOMY The science of the stars, planets, and all other heavenly bodies, which studies their composition, motion, relative position, and size.

BAGHDAD A city on the Tigris River in present-day Iraq that was once the caliphate city in southwest Asia.

BEDOUIN Peoples of the nomadic desert tribes of Arabia, Syria, and North Africa.

BERBERS Pre-Arab inhabitants of North Africa, scattered in tribes across the mountains and deserts of Morocco, Algeria, Tunisia, Libya, and Egypt.

BYZANTINE EMPIRE The eastern part of the Roman Empire, with its capital at Byzantium (the city later renamed Constantinople, and now Istanbul).

CALIPH The title taken by Muhammad's successors as the leaders of Islam.

CALIPHATE The rank or reign of a caliph; the lands ruled by a caliph.

CALLIGRAPHY The art of decorative, stylized writing.

CARAVAN A group of travelers, often merchants or pilgrims, traveling together for safety.

CONSTANTINOPLE The ancient city of Byzantium that was the capital of the east Roman Empire, was renamed after the emperor Constantine, and fell to the Ottomans in 1453; now Istanbul.

CRUSADES A series of campaigns by western European Christian armies to recapture the Holy Land from the Muslims; eight major Crusades took place between 1095 and 1291.

DAMASCUS A city in Syria.

DHIMMIS Non-Muslims living in Islamic regions whose rights are protected by the state.

DHOW A single-masted ship with a triangular sail, sharp prow, and raised deck at the stern.

DOME OF THE ROCK Qubbat al-Sakhra, a shrine in Jerusalem built in about 688–691, on a site that is sacred to Muslims and Jews; one of the oldest examples of Islamic architecture still standing.

FAJR The first prayer of the day, before sunrise.

FASTING To abstain from all or certain foods.

FIVE PILLARS OF ISLAM The five core requirements of practising Islam: *iman, salat, zakat, sawm,* and *hajj.*

Minarets make a stunning skyline

Cairo, Egypt, founded by the Fatimid caliphate

FRANKINCENSE A gum resin obtained from trees in Arabia and northeast Africa; burned as incense.

GABRIEL The Archangel; the messenger of God who revealed the Quran to Muhammad.

HADITH An account of the Prophet Muhammad's life; a collection of Muhammad's sayings.

HAFIZ A person who has committed the text of the Quran to memory.

HAJJ The pilgrimage to the Islamic holy city of Mecca in Saudi Arabia. It includes a series of rites over several days and is one of the Five Pillars of Islam.

HALAL Food that is lawful for Muslims to eat under their dietary rules.

HIJAB The veil that is worn by some Muslim women.

HIJRAH Muhammad's migration from Mecca to Medina in 622, which marks the beginning of the Muslim era and the Muslim calendar.

HOLY LAND A historic name given by Christians to Palestine and Israel.

IHRAM The special state of holiness that pilgrims must achieve before making a pilgrimage; also the special clothing that Muslims wear on a pilgrimage to Mecca.

IKAT A technique that involves tie-dyeing threads before weaving to create bold, colorful textiles; also the textile that is produced using this method.

IMAM A prayer leader; may also provide community support and spiritual advice.

IMAN Faith; one of the Five Pillars of Islam.

ISHA The last prayer of the day, in the evening.

Bedouin travelers in a caravan

ISLAM A monotheistic religion founded by the Prophet Muhammad; its name means "submission" and comes from the Arabic word for "peace."

JABAL AL-NUR The Mountain of Light; the place near Mecca where Muhammad went to meditate during the month of Ramadan. The Quran was first revealed to him here, in a cave called Hira.

JULUS A stage in Muslim prayer; the sitting position.

KABA The ancient stone sanctuary dedicated to God, situated at the center of the Sacred Mosque in Mecca, where millions of pilgrims pray during the annual hajj.

KHUTBA The name for a sermon delivered by an imam.

KUFIC A bold, angular style of script that is used in Islamic calligraphy.

KURSI A wooden support used for holding a copy of the Quran.

MADRASA The Arabic word for school; historically, an Islamic center of higher education, often linked to a mosque, for the study of religion and law.

MAGHRIB The fourth prayer of the day, after sunset.

MECCA The birthplace of Muhammad; Islam's holiest city and a center of pilgrimage; in present-day Saudi Arabia.

MEDINA Muhammad's capital city, in present-day Saudi Arabia; the site of his tomb, and the second-holiest city in Islam after Mecca.

MIHRAB An often-elaborate niche in the wall of a mosque, indicating the direction to Mecca.

MINARET The highest point of a mosque, from which the call to prayer is given.

MINBAR A raised pulpit in a mosque, where the imam stands to give a sermon.

MONGOLS Nomadic people of Central Asia, originally from the steppes of Mongolia, who invaded much of the Islamic world in the 13th century and made many conquests under the leadership of Genghis Khan and his successors.

MOSQUE In Islam, the place of worship; a building specifically used for prayer and open for prayer throughout the week.

Intricately carved mosque doors

MUHAMMAD The Prophet and founder of Islam, born in Mecca in the year 570, to whom Gabriel revealed messages from God. These formed the Quran, which was memorized by his closest followers, the Companions, and written down shortly after his death in 632.

MUEZZIN In Islam, the person who sounds the call to prayer.

MULLAH A person who is learned in religion. Most mullahs have had formal religious training.

Prayer mat with mosque design

MUSHAF Literally, a collection of pages; a copy of the Quran.

NOMAD A member of a tribe or people which has no permanent home, but which moves about constantly.

OASIS A fertile place in a desert due to a source of water.

OTTOMAN EMPIRE Islamic empire established in Anatolia (Asia Minor) in the late 13th century.

PERSIA The name for the Middle Eastern nation that is now Iran.

PILGRIMAGE See hajj.

PRAYER MAT A small rug used by many followers of Islam for prayer.

QIBLA The direction of Mecca toward which Muslims pray.

QURAN The holy book of Islam; the word of God, as revealed to Muhammad. This name usually refers to the book that has the Quran written in it; originally, it referred to the words themselves, which Muslims had to learn by heart.

RAKA In Muslim prayer, the motion of bowing down to show respect for Allah.

RAMADAN The ninth month in the Muslim year, observed by Muslims as a month of fasting, called *sawm*.

SALAT The regular daily prayers in Islam said five times a day; one of the Five Pillars of Islam.

SALAM The final stage in daily prayer; the peace.

SAWM The name for the fast during the month of Ramadan; one of the Five Pillars of Islam.

SELJUKS Nomadic Turkish peoples who began to spread southward in the 11th century, capturing Baghdad.

SHAHADA In Islam, a profession of faith.

SHARIA The name for the holy law of Islam, compiled and codified in the 8th and 9th centuries.

SURA One of the 114 chapters in the Quran, the holy book.

TIRAZ Specially made cloth woven with calligraphic designs.

TURKS A general name for central Asian peoples of nomadic origin.

UMRAH Part of the annual hajj, performed on arrival in Mecca; also a minor pilgrimage at any time of year.

WAQF A gift given to the state for good works such as building a mosque.

Zakat is usually paid with cash

ZAKAT A tax that is paid as a percentage of a person's wealth, which is distributed among the poor and needy; one of the Five Pillars of Islam.

ZUHR The noon prayer; on Fridays, Muslim men are required to gather for the midday prayer.

The Alhambra Palace

The fortified palace of the Alhambra in Granada, Spain, is made up of stunning halls, courtyards surrounded by arched walkways, and tranquil gardens. The Palace of the Lions, shown here, is decorated with dazzling geometric patterns and fine Arabic script.